MODELLING
US World War II
Armoured Fighting Vehicles

MODELLING
US World War II
Armoured Fighting Vehicles

Tom Cole

THE CROWOOD PRESS

First published in 2022 by
The Crowood Press Ltd
Ramsbury, Marlborough
Wiltshire SN8 2HR

enquiries@crowood.com

www.crowood.com

British Library Cataloguing-in-Publication Data
A catalogue record for this book is available from the British Library.

ISBN 978 0 7198 4027 2

Typeset by Simon and Sons
Cover design by Blue Sunflower Creative
Printed and bound in India by Parksons Graphics

Contents

Dedication

For Max.

Photo Credits

Photographs by Alex Cossey and the author. Majority of models by the author with 1/35 scale models by Simon Ward.

Chapter 1

Introduction and Choosing Your Scale

This is the third book in the military modelling series from The Crowood Press. The first title by Robin Buckland examined modelling German Armoured Fighting Vehicles (AFVs) of World War II and the second title, by this author, discussed British AFVs in the same period. This third title will consider all the AFVs from the United States of America (abbreviated to 'USA/US' for convenience throughout the book), from December 1941 to the end of hostilities against Japan in August 1945.

There are numerous books and articles on modelling US armoured vehicles, but most of these cover only the most popular scale of 1/35. This book will focus on the smaller scales of 1/76, 1/72 and 1/48 – scales that, with only a few exceptions, are seldom covered in any depth in modelling magazines or even online. The bibliography at the end of this book includes details of other books that may be of interest to the reader.

A SHORT HISTORY OF MILITARY MODELMAKING

Human beings have made small replicas of buildings and people since the dawn of time. However, a major explosion in the modelmaking industry took place in the 1960s, when plastics became cheap and readily available. Leading the charge, in the UK at least, was the modelmaking company Airfix. Such was the firm's popularity that teenagers of the 1960s and 1970s are sometimes referred to as the 'Airfix Generation'.

Airfix's biggest range was, and still is, 1/72nd-scale aircraft – although the complete Airfix range originally included historical figures, small-scale sailing ships, vintage cars, plastic soldiers and model railway buildings and rolling stock. In 1960 the first Airfix military vehicle appeared in the form of the Bristol Bloodhound Surface-to-Air Missile kit. The first Airfix armoured fighting vehicles were released in 1961 as the Panther, Sherman and Churchill tank kits. Sixty years on, these kits are still available. The military vehicle range would never rival the Airfix aircraft range, but small-scale vehicles were produced by other manufacturers, such as Japanese Fujimi and Nitto and Italian Esci. Then, in 1972, British company Matchbox introduced a range of AFVs in 1/76 scale that filled some of the many gaps that existed in the Airfix range.

Whilst small-scale military models in 1/76 and 1/72 scales dominated the 1960s and early 1970s, the revolution that would change the face of military modelmaking saw its beginning in 1962 when the Japanese firm Tamiya introduced their first large-scale AFV. The 1/35th-scale Panther was a success, but the product was a curious hybrid between a toy and a serious modelmaking kit. It included an electric motor and could move around the living room in a reasonably accurate fashion. However, by 1968 the Panther had been supplemented by a series of figures that included

COLLECTOR OR WARGAMER?

People normally construct model vehicles either because they want to build a collection of models or they want to use them on a Wargames table. The bigger-scale models (1/35 and 1/48) are currently the most popular for collectors and smaller scales (1/56 and 1/72) are more often the province of wargamers. However, some wargamers choose to run around with 1/16-scale radio-controlled tanks and many collectors prefer to model in 1/72 and 1/76. So, there are no hard and fast rules. Much depends on budget and storage when deciding scale. Apart from scale, the main difference between wargamers and collectors is the obvious one. Wargame models must be robust and strong enough to be frequently handled, not just on the miniature battlefield but when they are in transit between games. Collectors go for fine detail, knowing that their models will spend most of their time on a shelf or in a display case (or sadly in a box in the loft), and may occasionally be transported to be shown off at a model show or exhibition. Some wargamers will be content with the quick-build 'snap together' kits that are more popular now than ever before, but some will choose to build their models with a level of detail that some collectors would envy. Modelmaking is as individual as the individuals that make models.

German soldiers and tank crew. The range rapidly expanded and 1/35 scale became the dominant scale for military modellers. This is still the case today.

Currently, the military modelling market has never been stronger. The range of model kits in all scales is the largest and most comprehensive it has ever been. Airfix have entered the 1/35 market with several models that originated from other makers and they occasionally release a new small-scale AFV kit, but their range is limited compared to the flood of small-scale models that regularly appear from all parts of the world – particularly Russia, Ukraine and Poland, as well as South Korea

and China. Some companies normally associated with large-scale models such as Dragon Models produce small-scale kits that are as realistic-looking as their bigger-scale versions.

CHOOSING YOUR SCALE

If you are new to military modelling, one of the first things you should think about is the scale in which you are going to build your models. Some modellers choose to model in a variety of scales, but most have a favourite scale and seldom stray from it. I have always made small-scale models, predominately 1/76 and 1/72, but have recently re-discovered the joy of 1/48 scale.

Very small scales

Probably the smallest models available are in 1/700 scale. This is a popular scale for ship modellers and the tiny vehicles in this scale are often used as loads for ship landing craft. Predominately models in 1/300 and 1/285 are used for wargaming. Normally cast in white metal, these tiny models from companies such as GHQ are manufactured to a very high standard when you consider that the figures used are only 6mm tall. Models in 1/144 and 1/150 equate to railway N gauge. Whilst they fit in well with the ever-growing range of 1/144-scale aircraft, the range of kits available is limited – although Revell have produced one set of vehicles in this small scale that are relevant to the US Army in World War II.

Small scale

A scale that is popular for wargaming has figures that are 15mm high and equates to 1/100. The Plastic Soldier Company produces a large range of vehicles and figures. Russia-based firm Zvezda also produce simplified vehicles in this scale as part of their 'Art of Tactic' wargame. Many of the military vehicle scales can trace their roots in railway modelling and 1/87 is the dominant model railway scale in Europe. It is also known as HO, but 1/87 has never been that popular in the UK. Another

This Sherman depicts a tank in use with the US Marines in the Pacific and is in 1/72 scale. The basic kit has been extensively modified to represent the modifications that the US Marines applied to many of their tanks.

scale that has its origins in the model railway range equates to 4mm to the foot or 'OO' gauge. This is 1/76. Airfix produced their range of military vehicles in 1/76 to go with their range of figures and model railways, rather than 1/72, which is their main aircraft scale. The dominant manufacturers were Airfix and Matchbox (with Revell now running some of the original Matchbox kits alongside their 1/72 range). Japan-based Fujimi and Nitto produced military vehicle kits in 1/76, but the majority of small-scale kits are in 1/72 scale. This is by far the most popular of the smaller scales. The 1/72 kits from one of the early manufacturers, Esci, emerged a little after the early Airfix kits and set the standard for small-scale modelling. That tradition of high-quality kits has continued with the major manufacturers Revell, Dragon and Italeri producing some incredibly detailed kits in 1/72, some of which date back to the early days of Esci. Some manufacturers have produced military vehicles in this scale aimed at the wargamer. These tend to have two 'snap-together' kits in the box, with the emphasis being on a sturdy model that can withstand frequent handling on the wargames table, rather than having large amounts of fine detail. Zvezda have bucked that particular trend by producing wargames models that are both robust and yet highly detailed.

Medium scales

Another scale similar to 1/100 that is aimed at the wargames market is 1/56. This scale is also known as 28mm, as this is the height of the figures from floor- to eye-level. Kits from the major manufacturers such as Italeri tend to be simplified. For example, suspension units and tracks are produced as a single item.

Known as 'Quarter Scale', 1/48 is a very popular scale for model aircraft manufacturers. Bandai

The T31 Demolition Tank never entered production but makes an interesting model. This particular model is in 1/56 scale. This scale is popular with wargamers.

Compared to 1/72 and 1/35 there are relatively few kits available in 1/48 scale. This US Marine Corps M4A3 is a heavily modified kit from HobbyBoss. A 3D-printed Japanese Tankette is in the foreground.

produced some highly detailed AFV kits in the 1970s and Tamiya have a reasonable range of military vehicles from various nations. However, 1/48 is not as popular as 1/72 or 1/35. This issue has been partially addressed by some great models from Accurate Armour, but like many of the Tamiya kits, they are mainly soft-skins based around aircraft subjects. However, 1/48 scale is a good compromise; models in this scale are more detailed than 1/72 but do not take up the space of 1/35-scale models and are certainly cheaper, although the range of vehicles is limited.

Large scale

Known by some as the 'Standard Size', 1/32 scale is popular amongst model soldier collectors and is also known as 54mm. Airfix have produced a small number of military models in this scale, but it is an odd scale that does not have a big following. By far the most popular scale for military modelling is 1/35. This scale was not based on a deliberate decision but came about because Tamiya wanted to fit an electric motor and a 'C' type battery pack in a tank chassis. Their first military model – the Panther – was released in 1961. The scale grew in popularity in the 1970s

and now totally dominates the market. New manufacturers in this scale regularly appear – particularly from the Far East and eastern Europe. The vast array of kits in this scale covers just about every vehicle and variant that ever existed and this makes it a very attractive scale. Perhaps the only drawbacks are the space that completed models take up when compared to the smaller scales, and the relatively high price of many kits in 1/35 scale. Tamiya produced some tanks in 1/24 scale and there are specialist manufacturers such as Kit Form Services that produce some highly detailed kits in this large scale.

Very large scale

Tamiya and Trumpeter produce some military vehicles in 1/16 scale. Some are fully motorized, but generally these kits are expensive (Tamiya Panzer IV sells at around £500), so probably not the best choice if you are starting out in the hobby. For around £100 you can buy a remote-control, ready-to-run tank. Built for rugged handling, they are not as detailed as those from traditional kit manufacturers but they are proving popular. Those old enough will remember the 12in-tall Action Man figures. This equated to 1/6 scale

The most popular scale for military modelling is 1/35 scale. This tank destroyer shows the level of detail that can be achieved in this scale.

and, although you could buy a hard plastic tank for these figures, the latest iterations in this scale are very different from those toys of the 1960s. If you have a big budget or just want to make a once-in-a-lifetime purchase, then this might be the scale for you. Kits cost around £5,000 each and are fully motorized and remote controlled. Made from aluminium, brass and steel, assembly is relatively straightforward using household tools.

MODELLING MEDIUMS

Regardless of scale, the biggest range of military models available is plastic injection-moulded kits. These kits are provided in various degrees of complexity. Small-scale injection-moulded kits are either simple kits for wargamers or highly detailed kits for the more serious modelmaker. Large-scale kits can have literally hundreds of parts.

This M12 Gun Motor Carriage is a 1/48-scale resin kit from Gaso.line. It requires a chassis and the Tamiya M4 kit was used. Extra detailing comes from photo-etched parts and plastic card has been used to replace some of the more fragile resin parts. A truly multi-media kit.

Resin kits are normally available as limited runs from small 'cottage industry' providers. Small-scale resin kit manufacturers such as Geisbers Models, Milicast and Matador Models each have an enormous range of small-scale vehicles – mainly in 1/76 scale. Resin kits come in a variety of styles. Some are cast as a single AFV, mainly for the war-games market, whilst others have as many parts as the more complex injection-moulded kits. In the larger scales, resin tends to be used to provide conversion kits for injection-moulded kits. Resin is a popular medium for figure modelling in all scales.

Ready-assembled, die-cast metal models have often in the past been dismissed by serious model-makers as nothing more than toys. However, some of the recent offerings from Oxford Die-casts, Panzerstahl and Hobby Master, as well as models from kit manufacturers such as Dragon, are of a very high stand both in construction and in finish. Mainly small-scale examples can also be found in 1/35 scale. At one time there were some kit manu-facturers that provided models in white metal (a soft, easy-to-cast alloy), but now this medium is increasingly rare. Figures in white metal in various scales are still available from a few sources.

Some high-end models come complete with etched-brass detailing parts and perhaps a turned-brass gun barrel. This is by far the most popular medium for aftermarket detailing kits. Modellers who prefer the smaller scales are the poor relations compared to those that model in the larger scales when it comes to detailing sets. It seems that almost every kit in the large scale has at least one accompanying photo-etch and or resin detailing set, and for every plastic gun barrel in 1/35 there seems to be a turned-brass replacement. In the small scales there are detailing sets and gun bar-rels available, but these are the exception rather than the rule. Companies such as Hauler, ARMO, Extratech, Dan Taylor Modelworks and PART pro-duce a variety of detailing and conversion parts and Aber and RB produce some splendid turned-brass barrels in small scale, but not in the diversity that are produced for 1/35 scale.

Just as the home computer and smartphones have revolutionized all of our lives, so the 3D printer is thought by some to be the next big thing that will find a place in every home. However, 3D printing has yet to take off seriously. The quality of the finished item is generally poor and the cost of a good 3D printer is prohibitively high, but good-quality and inexpensive 3D printers may be with us all very soon. There are already a few 3D-printed models available from a variety of sources, but generally the best-quality models are expensive compared to resin or plastic alternatives. However, this may all change with improvements in technology and prices will eventually fall to meet those of resin and plastic models.

Chapter 2

A Short History of US Armour in World War II

INTRODUCTION

Whilst this book is focused on modelling US Army armoured vehicles of World War II, most modelmakers wish to know about the history and development of the vehicles they build so that they can give their models an historical context. The story of how the real vehicles of the USA developed before and during World War II is fascinating. Living at a time when the armed forces of the United States of America are the largest and most potent in the world, it is incredible to think that at the outbreak of World War II the US Army had as few as 174,000 of all ranks and was classified as only nineteenth in the world, slightly ahead of Bulgaria but firmly behind Portugal in terms of manpower. By 1945, US Army strength had grown to 8,267,958 with a strong emphasis on armoured forces. This was an incredible increase that took the USA from a minor armed force to centre stage as a leading world power in less than six years.

North America, along with much of Europe, suffered during the Great Depression and, as inevitably happens at times of recession, spending on armed forces after World War I was drastically cut. These cuts severely affected the US armoured forces. The end of World War I not unnaturally meant a drastic culling of armed forces, and the fledgling US armoured forces suffered particularly,

as mechanized forces were expensive. In July 1919 Congress declared that the US Tank Corps would be limited to no more than 154 officers and 2,508 other ranks. The tank corps lost its independent status and came under the control of the infantry. The concept was that in any future conflict tanks would be used only to provide support to the infantry. However, some serving tank corps officers (notably Lieutenant Colonel Dwight D. Eisenhower and Major George S. Patton) argued that the armoured forces should retain independence from the infantry and be under the control of the cavalry. This view was not supported by the top-ranked General of the Armies of the United States. John J. Pershing ensured that the National Defense Act of 1920 placed all tanks and their units under the control of the infantry. Inevitably, subordination of armoured forces to the infantry stifled tank design and doctrine, which would have repercussions in the next war and indeed beyond.

THE EMF

Despite these constraints, and inspired by combined arms exercises in Britain, the US Army formed the Experimental Mechanized Force (EMF) at the end of 1927. The EMF consisted of a headquarters company, an armoured car troop, a

© JOHN WOOLFORD

The M3 Light Tank was known as the Stuart or 'Honey' by the British. This example is at the Bovington Tank Museum being displayed at 'Tank Fest' in a rather gaudy scheme depicting a tank in British 8th Army service.

company of tanks, a machine-gun company and a self-propelled artillery battery, all supported by an engineer company, supply, signal, and chemical warfare troops. The Mechanization Board was set up in May 1928 and recommended that a permanent mechanized force be formed. This force went against the spirt of the 1920 Act, as it established that the role of armour was to carry out what were traditionally typical cavalry actions of scouting and exploitation. The infantry countered with a plan for establishing a tank division for each of the six field armies. The plan placed armour firmly under Infantry Command and not surprisingly was opposed by Chief of Cavalry, Major General Guy Henry via Major George Patton. The squabble was resolved by Army Chief of Staff General Douglas MacArthur dissolving the Mechanized

Force as a separate entity and ordering all combat branches to modernize as much as possible. This was the green light for the cavalry to explore mechanization.

By 1932 the infantry had the **Light Tank T2** and the cavalry the **Combat Car T5**. Both were tanks, but because under the 1920 Act only the infantry could have tanks, the cavalry had to use the subterfuge of a combat car. The T2 and T5 had a common ancestry and shared the same chassis and many parts. They would evolve into a whole series of **Light Tanks M3 and M5** that would see active service throughout World War II with the US Army, US Marines and numerous allies. The remnants of the dissolved EMF were assigned to the cavalry to become the Mechanized Cavalry Regiment. Originally based at Camp Knox in western Kentucky in late 1931, this would become Fort Knox the next year and the home of US armour for almost 80 years.

MEDIUM TANKS

Parallel to the development of the light tanks, the US Tank Board looked to North American industry to provide medium tanks. No history of American armour would be complete without reference to the eccentric J. Walter Christie. The suspension system that bore his name featured large road wheels individually sprung on leading or trailing arms suspended on soft helical springs that were housed inside a double-walled hull. This revolutionary suspension was combined with the novel concept of the vehicle using wheels when travelling on roads but tracks when going cross country. In both modes the vehicle travelled fast and smooth. Unfortunately Christie's prototype tanks had a reputation for shoddy workmanship and were generally unreliable, which resulted in some dismal trials. Some Christie designs (the **Medium T1** for the infantry and **Combat Car T1** for the cavalry) saw small production runs and the Americans continued to toy with the Christie design between 1930 and 1936 with the **T2, T3, T3E2 and T4**, but Christie's designs were generally dismissed in his home country. However, he fared better overseas, with Britain adopting the Christie suspension for their medium tanks and the Soviets taking the Christie suspension to produce the BT Series of tanks, which would be developed into arguably the best tank of World War II – the T34. (It is a matter of speculation as to what the outcome would have been if the Americans had persisted with the Christie design, but perhaps it would have led to the US Army possibly being equipped with a T34 type tank rather than the M4 Sherman.)

Rather than follow the Christie design, US armour development favoured the volute suspension system (a volute spring is a compression spring in the form of a cone), used in the **M2 light tanks**, which had been designed by Harry A. Knox in the early 1920s. Knox filed dozens of patents related to mechanization, but his most important were volute spring suspension and tracks with rubber bushings around the track pins. This suspension would see widespread use throughout US armour. Most Light Tanks, all Medium Tanks and

even the **M6 Heavy Tank** all used either vertical or horizontal volute suspension systems. The US ordnance department's Rock Island arsenal produced the **T5 Medium Tank** in 1938 and this would lead to development of the **Medium M2 and M2A1 Tanks**. These all carried the same 37mm gun used on the M2 Light Tank. However, the Medium M2 was much larger, and when the German Wehrmacht swept through most of Europe, analysis by Chief of Infantry Brigadier General Asa L. Singleton advised the ordnance department that the Medium Tank M2 should be improved to match the German Panzerkampwagen IV that carried a 75mm gun.

Although the USA was still neutral at this juncture, it was clearly only a matter of time as to when they would enter the war against Germany. Singleton's need for a tank that could match the German Panzer IV was echoed by the British army, whose tanks were generally unreliable and poorly armed (most British tanks carried a 2pdr gun that was only slightly superior to the US 37mm gun). British tanks were struggling to defeat the

WHAT'S IN A NAME?

American tanks were numbered following a strict system of designation. Prototype or trials AFVs were given the prefix T and production vehicles had the letter M. The official title had a letter followed by a number with a description. Hence, the M3 Light Tank was a very different vehicle to the M3 Medium Tank. The British had an even more complex method of naming their armour, but were fond of giving their tanks names – Matilda and Comet, for example. When tanks from the USA appeared in their armoury, the British named them after US civil war generals. So the M3 Light Tank became the General Stuart and the M3 Medium Tank became the General Grant for the version modified for the British and the General Lee for those in use by US armoured forces (although a few Lee tanks did find their way into British hands). The 'General' prefix was normally dropped: for example, the M4 Medium Tank was best known as the Sherman. The Americans never really adopted the names given by the British but did unofficially use names like 'Hellcat' for the M18 Tank Destroyer. For AFVs other than tanks, the nomenclature was based on the armament of the vehicle. Gun motor carriages carried a gun as opposed to a Howitzer motor carriage. Hence the M12 Gun Motor Carriage carried a 155 mm gun and the M7 Howitzer Motor Carriage carried a 105mm howitzer. (The British followed a strange tradition of naming their self-propelled guns after clergy and would give the M7 HMC the name 'Priest'.) 'Multiple Gun Motor Carriages' was the term used for the various AFVs that mounted two or more guns, normally in an anti-aircraft role. The names given to US tanks have long since entered general use, although some are not so well known. I recently discovered that the M8 Howitzer Motor Carriage is named after General Winfield Scott.

better-armed German tanks in the North African Western Desert. With great urgency, the US ordnance board looked for a quick means of mounting a 75mm gun in the M2 Medium. By a twist of fate, a suitable arrangement that mounted a 75mm field gun in a sponson of a surplus M2 Medium had been under evaluation since April 1939. The resulting **Medium Tank M3** retained a 37mm in a turret like the Medium M2 but carried a more powerful 75mm gun in a side sponson. At best this was an interim measure, but when shipments of the M3 Medium – built to British specifications and named the General Grant – arrived in the Western Desert, the tank was found to be the equal of the best German tanks and better than most German and Italian armour. The Grant was the first tank in the British armoury that could fire both armour-piercing and high-explosive shells, and so at last British armour could take on enemy infantry and anti-tank guns at battle ranges.

Although initially a success, the unusual arrangement of locating the main weapon in a side sponson was not without drawbacks. One of

the principal tactics used by all sides in the Western Desert was to fight from a 'Hull Down' position. This involved positioning a tank on the reverse slope of a hill so that only the turret was exposed. However, the Grant could not fire its 75mm gun in such a position and not being able to rotate the main gun through 360 degrees proved to be a serious tactical disadvantage on a battlefield where the action was often fast moving. As the M3 was coming off the production lines, development was already underway to build its replacement with the 75mm gun mounted in a suitable turret. The new **M4 Medium Tank** (referred to as the Sherman by the British) was based very much on the M3 with the same volute suspension and the same 75mm gun. Desperate for more new and effective armour the British received, under the new Lend-Lease agreement, the new M4A1 Sherman tanks to supplement the Grants at the second battle of El Alamein in October 1942.

The British Sherman's debut showed that the Allies had a tank superior to most German tanks and at least on a par with the Panzer IV 'Special',

The M3 Medium, known by the British as the 'General Grant', with the US version called the 'Lee'. When first introduced the Grant gave the British their first tank capable of firing a reasonable anti-tank or high-explosive round. But the 75mm gun in a sponson was at best a compromise measure.

This splendidly restored M4A1 clearly shows the cast hull of the first production Sherman. Also prominent is the three-piece transmission case that was replaced on later models with a single-piece cast nose.

The M4 Sherman painted up in British colours and referred to by the British as the Sherman I. This example carries a 0.3in-calibre anti-aircraft machine gun on the turret, which was common practice for US vehicles.

© JOHN WOOLFORD

with its long-barrelled 75mm gun. However, the US Ordnance Department were aware that they had now entered an arms race against the Germans. Rumours of new and far more powerful German tanks became a reality when the first Tiger tanks appeared in Tunisia. Plans for the M4

Medium's replacement were being considered as the first Shermans were entering production. The Sherman's turret front plate was interchangeable, and it was planned to replace the 75mm gun with a 105mm howitzer for infantry support and install a 3in gun M7 to improve the Sherman's ability to defeat the expected next generation of German tanks. The 105mm-armed M4 did eventually enter service, but the 3in gun proved difficult to fit in the Sherman turret (although the 3in M7 was successfully fitted in the M6 Heavy Tank and used in anger when fitted in the **GMC M10** Tank Destroyer). The Sherman would eventually be armed with a higher-velocity gun in the form of the 76mm M1 and M1A1 guns, but this would be as a result of the failure of the **T23 tank** project (see below). In June 1944 it was intended to field 75mm and 76mm gun tanks in a ratio of two-thirds to one-third. Combat experience showed the value of the 76mm gun and by the time of the Rhine crossings in March 1945, approximately 40 per cent of the Shermans in the European theatre stocks were armed with the 76mm gun.

One of the plans to replace the M4 Medium would emerge from the development of the **T7 Light Tank**, which in turn had been proposed as the replacement for the M2 and M3 Light Tanks. The **M7 Medium** took the T7 and replaced the 57mm gun with a 75mm gun in a new turret. This almost doubled the weight of the tank from 14 tons to 25 tons. Although a contract had been placed with the International Harvester Company in December 1942 to produce 3,000 M7 Medium tanks, trials of the pilot model showed that the new tank was grossly underpowered. Plans to replace the engine with a more powerful Ford V8 were shelved as the **M4A3 Medium** was entering production and even with a new engine the M7 had inferior performance compared to the latest Sherman. Neither the T7 nor M7 ever entered production.

A more successful project was the T20 series of tanks, which commenced in the spring of 1942. The development work for a new tank culminated in the **T23 Medium Tank** that featured an electric drive train to the drive sprockets, which were mounted at the rear next to the engine. This meant that, unlike the Sherman, there was no drive shaft from engine to drive sprockets and so the T23 could have a much lower silhouette than the M4 Medium, giving the T23 a significant

tactical advantage. The T23 also came with a high-velocity 76mm gun in a large turret at a time when the M4 could only be fitted with a lower-velocity 75mm gun. In May 1943 procurement of 250 of the T23 was authorized and these models were built between November 1943 and December 1944, although the tank would never enter service. Concern was expressed by the Armored Force Board that the tank's weight distribution and excessive ground pressure, coupled with a drive system that was not proven, presented too great a risk. The 250 completed vehicles were offered up for delivery to Europe, but the Army considered that supporting two different medium tanks in theatre would result in significant logistical issues for what was seen as little advantage.

The T23 Medium was doomed never to enter service. Yet the tank made a significant contribution to American tank design, as the T23 turret with the 76mm gun fitted the M4 Sherman with only a few changes and so became the standard turret for the later versions of the Sherman. In addition, the development work on the T23 would lead to the development of the T26, which would go into service in Europe in the closing stages of World War II. It could be seen that the T23 was the best tank the US Armoured Forces never had. The thick sloping front armour, 76mm gun and torsion-bar suspension of the later version (T23 E3) had the look of the German Panther and may have given US tankers parity with that tank – but it was not to be.

Combat experience meant that, by May 1943, there was interest in arming a medium tank with the new 90mm tank gun. Forty of the T23 hulls were modified with a torsion bar suspension, given a more conventional powertrain and fitted with a 90mm gun turret. Designated **T25E1**, ten similar tanks were built with thicker armour to become the **T26E1**. Testing in 1944 led to revisions to ammunition stowage, transmission and brakes with the improved version named T26E3 seeing combat in Europe in February 1945. Further improvements led to the **M26 Heavy Tank**, which would be the mainstay of American armour

The M26 Heavy Tank arrived in the final months of World War II in small numbers and at last gave the US Army a tank equal to the German Tiger and Panthers. This post-war version is in a Belgium military museum.

in the Korean War and the later **M48 and M60 tanks** such as the M26 could trace their lineage back to the T23.

HEAVY TANKS

The M26 Heavy Tank was not the first heavy tank that the US Ordnance Department had considered. Thought had been given to the development of a heavy tank as early as October 1940. At 50 tons, the **Heavy Tank T1** would have 75mm frontal armour with a turret that mounted co-axially a 3in and 37mm gun. Development of the heavy tank continued and culminated with what would be termed the **M6A2 Heavy Tank**. But trials of this tank showed that the M6A2 was unsatisfactory, being too heavy, under-gunned, a poor ballistic shape and featuring a transmission that had significant problems. Further development was carried out, but the M6 in any form would never

enter mass production and by December 1944 the M6 series was declared obsolete.

LIGHT TANKS

Whilst medium tanks made up the majority of armour used by the US Army in World War II, one-third of tanks in a Tank Division in 1944 were light tanks. The **M2 Light Tank** was superseded by the **M3 and M3A1 Light Tanks** (Stuart or 'Honey' in British hands), which in turn would be replaced by the **M5 and M5A1 Light Tanks**. All of these different versions of the light tank were adapted to different roles but their main task would always be scouting and reconnaissance. The US Army love of the light tank culminated in the **M24 Chaffee**, which carried the 75mm M6 gun that was the same calibre as the main armament of the early M4 Medium. The Americans did produce a light tank capable of being air-lifted. The **M22 Light**

M24 Light Tank. The Americans persisted with light tanks and the Chaffee arrived in the European theatre in November 1944. Most Light Tank Companies in US Armored Divisions were equipped with the M24 by the end of World War II.

Tank (Airborne) was known as the 'Locust' by the British, but was never used in combat by the US Army. However, a large number of M22s were provided under Lend-Lease to the British 6th Airborne Division, who used a small number of them carried in Hamilcar gliders for the Rhine crossing on 24 March 1945.

TANK DESTROYERS

The organizational change that began following exercises in August 1940 and the heavy influence of lessons shown by the German's Blitzkrieg tactics resulted in the concept of the Tank Destroyer. It was perceived that any breakthrough of the front line by massed ranks of enemy armour would be stopped by the deployment of fast, lightly-armoured but heavily-armed AFVs. These tank destroyers would be held in readiness behind the front line and swoop into action as required. Speed and high mobility were achieved at the expense of armour. Open-topped turrets and thin armour all round made them vulnerable to shell splinters and all but the lightest of small arms. However, the whole tank destroyer concept was flawed, as by the time the Americans deployed

them, the Germans tended to attack with small arms teams and not deploy armour en masse. As the war progressed, the Germans simply did not have the resources for massed tank attacks.

The tank destroyer's debut in Tunisia was a disaster, as it was impossible to use the new vehicle offensively, as intended. However, tactical doctrine and new tank destroyer designs forged ahead. The US Army's only purpose-built, self-propelled tank destroyer was the **M18 Gun Motor Carriage** (unofficially named the Hellcat) in July 1943. Interim designs based on existing vehicles, including the 37mm-armed **M6 GMC**, 75mm-armed **M3 GMC** and the 3in-armed **M10** filled the gap and supported towed anti-tank guns of similar calibres. The advent of more powerfully-armed tanks and the poor initial performance of tank destroyer battalions led to confidence in the concept waning. However, the 90mm-armed **M36 GMC Jackson** was the most effective tank destroyer used by the US Army and it arrived in the European theatre of operations as the most heavily-armed AFV in the US Army, only equalled by the M26 Pershing when that tank arrived in the closing stages of World War II. Although they were never used in their intended role – as a counter to massed ranks of enemy tanks – the

The M18 tank destroyer was nicknamed the 'Hellcat'. Lightly armoured with an open-top turret, the M18 was very vulnerable to anything other than small arms fire, relying on speed for protection. Nevertheless, it acquitted itself well in combat.

© JOHN WOOLFORD

A beautifully restored M36 tank destroyer known as the 'General Jackson'. The 90mm gun was the most potent weapon used by the US Army in World War II and enabled the M36 to penetrate the thick armour of the later German tanks at battle ranges exceeding 500 metres.

various tank destroyers acquitted themselves well. At a time when even armed with a 76mm gun the Sherman struggled to defeat the new heavy German armour, the fast and manoeuvrable tank destroyers – particularly the 90mm-armed M36 – did much to improve the anti-tank capability of the US armoured divisions.

FURTHER INNOVATIONS

With an eye on the German success in 1939 and 1940 the Department of Field Artillery realized that traditional horse-drawn artillery was obsolete. The general concept was that the horse would be replaced by a tractor, but in some circles the concept of self-propelled mounts gathered favour. In early 1941 the Ordnance Department began work on a fully-tracked, self-propelled gun and the **T18 75mm Howitzer Motor Carriage** placed a M1A1 pack howitzer in an M3 Light Tank. However, the design was unsatisfactory and attention was switched to what would become the **M8 Howitzer Motor Carriage**. The T18 had demonstrated that combining an existing tank chassis with an in-service field artillery piece was a practical concept. With the chassis of a medium tank and the gun a heavier 105mm calibre, the **M7 Howitzer Motor Carriage** came to fruition. The first vehicles were finished in April 1942. The M7 gave the US Army artillery support that could keep pace with tanks and offer armoured protection to artillery crews – a factor that when compared like-for-like to towed artillery would halve the battle casualty rate.

© JOHN WOOLFORD

The M8 75mm Howitzer Motor Carriage was developed on the chassis of the M5 Stuart tank and was equipped with an M116 howitzer in an M7 mount.

As well as the 105mm howitzer, the US Army had a number of 155mm M1918 guns that were an old French design from World War I. Army Ground Forces initially rejected the T6 Motor Gun Carriage that fitted the M1918 in a Medium M3 chassis, but the ordnance department pushed on with development. Designated **M12 GMC**, an order for 100 vehicles was completed in March 1943. However, army ground forces clearly remained unconvinced of the value of the M12, as no more were ordered. Yet concerns about mobile artillery support to armoured forces meant that by December 1943, with invasion of Europe looming, seventy-four M12 which had been used for training in the USA, were overhauled and made ready for deployment and arrived in Europe just after the invasion. Despite only being available in small numbers, the M12s, acquitted itself well in both direct and indirect firing missions. Ultimately the M12 would be replaced by the **M40 GMC**, although only a few examples of this AFV were rushed to the European theatre as World War II ended.

The Pacific theatre is often overlooked when considering the impact of armour, yet both the US Army and US Marine Corps successfully deployed armour to the full in their Pacific campaigns. The army had standardized on the petrol-powered M4A3 Medium, which meant the marines could more quickly obtain large numbers of the diesel-powered **M4A2s** and they became the only US user of this version of the Sherman. The other armoured vehicle most closely associated with the USA in the Pacific campaign was the **Landing Vehicle Tracked** (LVT). First used as a swamp rescue vehicle in Florida's Everglades, the LVT became a crucial weapon in the war in the Pacific, as it developed into a series of tough island-hopping campaigns. Initially they were un-armoured and used to ferry stores from ship-to-shore, but their value as assault craft was quickly seen and the **LVT 3 and 4** series were altered by moving the engine forward and adding a rear ramp, as well as adding armour and extra armament. Some had 37mm or 75mm guns added to become amphibious tanks.

The 155mm Gun Motor Carriage M40 was a vehicle built on a widened and lengthened Medium Tank M4A3 chassis, but with a Continental engine and Horizontal Volute Spring Suspension. This vehicle is in the Imperial War Museum at Duxford.

© JOHN WOOLFORD

Finally, any review of the development of armoured forces of the US Army and Marine Corps would be incomplete unless we considered a vehicle that came to prominence in World War II and then quickly vanished from most of the armouries around the world just a few years later. The half-track was an attempt to combine the cross-country performance of a tracked vehicle with the road performance of a wheeled vehicle. The US Army used **M2, M2A1, M3, M3A1 and M3A2 Half-tracks** and the armies of her allies used **M5, M5A1 and M9A1 Half-tracks** extensively. Principally used as 'battle taxis', they also towed guns and mortars (81mm Mortar Carriers **M4, M4A1 and M21** and **4.2inch Mortar Carrier T21**), mounted anti-tank guns (75mm Gun Motor Carriage **M3, M3A1, T30 and T73**) as well as 57mm (Gun Motor Carriage T48). The half-track was also used to carry the 105mm howitzers (**T19 Howitzer Motor Carriage and T38**). In the anti-aircraft role there were numerous designs mounting machine guns and cannon (**Multiple Gun Motor Carriage M13, M14, M15, M15A1 M16 and M17**), the 40mm AAA gun (**Gun Motor Carriage T54, T59 and T68**). This was all in addition to numerous experimental vehicles that would not go beyond one or two prototypes.

© JOHN WOOLFORD

An M3A1 half-track being used by World War II re-enactors. The half-track sought to combine good cross-country performance with high speed on roads but was a compromise in both areas. As a concept, it was dropped after World War II in favour of fully-tracked infantry carriers.

The story of how the armoured force of the United States of America went from low in the world rankings in 1940 to world dominance alongside the Soviet Union after just five years is fascinating. Full of twists and turns, decisions were made at the time that would have an enormous impact on the US Army's conduct of World War II. We can speculate endlessly as to what the impact would have been on US armour had they adopted the Christie suspension. Would America have gone to war with its own version of the T34? What if the T23 Medium had been more acceptable to those making the decision about US armour? Would the much better T23 have replaced the Sherman and the M26 Heavy Tank been available much earlier in World War II to tame the German Tigers and Panthers? It took some time for the US Army to fully understand that with the introduction of the Tiger and Panther the German tanks were superior to allied tanks in terms of armour and killing power. Concepts and doctrine played a role in the decisions made at the time, but the ability of the USA to mass-produce tanks that, although inferior to the German tanks, would eventually overwhelm the enemy would be the most important factor. However, whilst superiority in numbers was a major factor, it was the bravery of the US Army AFV crews who went into battle, often knowing that their mounts were technically inferior to the enemy Tigers and Panthers, that most deserves our respect.

Chapter 3

Building Model Kits

INTRODUCTION

Building model kits has been a popular hobby since the 1960s. The basic principles of using polystyrene cement to weld plastic parts together has not changed much, unlike the variety of tools and different media available. It seems at times that a model is not complete unless etched-brass extras are added and the proliferation of after-market parts grows on an almost daily basis – certainly in the larger scales. This chapter demonstrates basic techniques that a beginner should find useful.

For most modelmakers the anticipation of opening the box to see what is sliding around inside a new kit is a fundamental part of the hobby. Whilst the internet carries countless reviews of new kits with a plethora of pictures of sprues, opening that box and examining the contents still gives a thrill to many of us.

Removing from the sprue

Once ready to build, the first act – after examining parts and glancing through instructions – is to separate the components from the sprue. In my

It is always a thrill to open a new kit. The models from Dragon are always well wrapped with sprues protected in individual plastic bags.

youth this involved twisting the part until it came off in your hand – although I recall that in desperation sometimes teeth may have been involved with some kits! However, this is the worst possible thing you can do. Instead, sharp cutters for cutting as close to the part as possible are absolutely essential. For the more delicate parts like tools and antenna, removing with cutters can put the part under tension and so the part could snap. A fine-bladed razor saw comes into its own for removing small parts from the sprue.

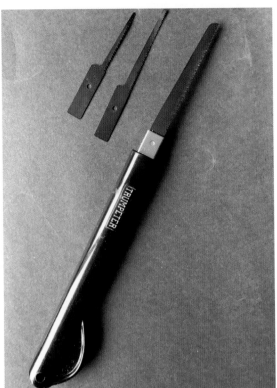

Razor saws are good for cutting delicate parts off the sprue and for cutting through thick plastic. This tool from Trumpeter comes with three different blades of varying teeth numbers per centimetre.

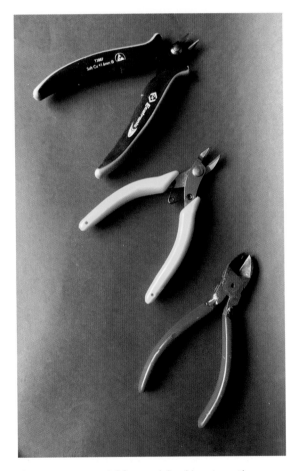

Cutters are essential for modelmaking. I use three pairs, mainly to cut parts off sprues. The red-handled pair are heavy duty for cutting thick plastic and the grey-handled cutters are very sharp for small parts, with the yellow-handled pair used for most other cutting. Cut as close as you can to the part to reduce the amount of sanding you need to do once the part is off the sprue.

Sanding sticks come in different grades. The higher the number means the finer the abrasive surface.

WHICH GLUE IS BEST?

When I first started modelmaking in the 1970s, when it came to glue there was not much choice. Polystyrene cement came in a tube (sometimes a thin *lead* tube – it seems incredible to think that lead tubes were commonplace then…) and you could buy two-part epoxy resin or contact adhesives. Today the range of different glues can be bewildering. The introduction of cyanoacrylate adhesive (CA) in the 1970s had an impact on the modelmaking world. Also known as 'superglue', the rapidity with which CAs set and their inherent strength meant that small parts can be easily held together and quickly. However, CAs are not always the best glue to use. Whilst they do set quickly this can be a disadvantage. Sometimes – particularly with large parts – you need to be able to slide the parts together to get the best fit. With a superglue you get 'one hit' – and if it is wrong you will need to break the join and start again. The other thing to consider is that generally a new application of superglue does not stick to old superglue – which means you have to scrape off the old glue before trying again. Today, there are specialist adhesives that can stick virtually anything to anything. The table below gives a guide to some of these.

Material 1	Material 2	Type of Glue	Example
Hard plastic	Hard plastic	Polystyrene	Tamiya Extra Thin Revell Contacta Professional
Hard plastic	Metal (small parts)	Cyanoacrylate adhesive	Gorilla Super Glue Gel
Hard plastic	Metal (large parts)	Epoxy resin	Araldite Rapid
Metal	Metal	Specialist epoxy resin	Araldite Metal
Resin	Resin (small parts)	Cyanoacrylate adhesive	Gorilla Super Glue Gel
Resin	Resin (large parts)	Epoxy resin	Araldite Rapid
Soft plastic	Soft plastic	Specialist glue	Bostick Soft Plastic – Clear
Clear plastic (windscreens)	Most others	Specialist glue	Humbrol Clearfix

Poly cement from Tamiya. The Extra Thin is particularly good for gluing small parts together.

CA superglues are available from numerous manufacturers. This Gorilla Glue is a gel and is ideal for cementing small parts of etched brass to plastic.

To ensure that the model does not end up covered in blobs of glue, apply the cement to the join inside the model.

Sanding and filing

The action of cutting the part from the sprue invariably leads to a small chunk of plastic from the sprue remaining behind. There are numerous sanding sticks available that can be used to clean up the part. For a metal part, such as a brass rod, a miniature metal file makes short work of any burrs.

Practise fitting

With the parts removed the next step is to practise the assembly of parts. This will show how well (or not) the parts come together and where the glue needs to be applied, as well as if any additional sanding is required to ensure a perfect fit.

Glues and adhesives

Whilst it is tempting to apply a big blob of glue to ensure the parts stick together, this is not the best way to go. Excess glue squeezed out between two parts can be difficult to remove and spoil the final result. When cementing large parts together, the best way is to hold or clamp the parts together and then run glue along the inside of the joint. Whilst

this is not always possible, as a general guide, applying glue where it cannot be seen yields the best results. The application of the glue can be a challenge. Squeezing glue out of a tube directly onto a part can lead to the part being swamped with glue. Many modern polystyrene cements come with a means of delivering small amounts of glue to the right place. This can be a brush fixed to the cap or via a thin tube like a hypodermic needle. You can buy specialist applicators that pick up a small amount of glue, allowing it to be applied precisely to the point needed. These are quite expensive and I have found that a cocktail stick can be just as effective and much cheaper.

Filling, sanding and scraping

Sanding tools come in a variety of grades and for plastic models medium (grades 240–400) and fine (grades 600–1,000) tend to be the most useful. You can buy sanding sticks in these grades or use sandpaper from a DIY store. The sanding sticks have a soft sponge backing and so are easier to use than sandpaper. There are special sanding tools from a variety of sources, but for plastic I

APPLICATION OF GLUE

The 'Touch-n-Flow' system is a trade name for a system that can be used to accurately apply a small amount of very thin liquid solvent cement. The applicator is a thin glass tube that ends with a very thin hollow needle. A squeezable bottle is fitted to the open end of the glass tube and the hollow needle immersed in a bottle of 'Plast-i-Weld' thin liquid cement. The bottle is then squeezed to evacuate the glass tube and when the squeezed bottle is released the liquid cement is drawn up through the needle into the glass tube. With the plastic bottle removed, the glue then flows through capillary action, as you draw the needle along the part you want to cement in place. The small bore nozzle allows for pin-point accuracy, with only tiny amounts of glue being released at a time.

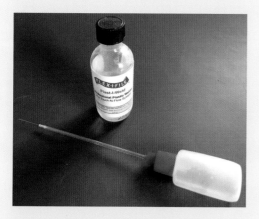

The Touch-N-Flow system is a good method for applying a small amount of glue in a precise position.

Sanding sticks are useful to get into tight spaces and corners.

with a specialist filler and then smoothing with fine sandpaper will get rid of any gaps and, if you have an overlap, then scraping a sharp blade along the seam will resolve the issue. You can buy a special tool such as a seam scraper, but it is probably not something a vehicle modeller will use much.

Drilling holes

Modern kits tend to have gun barrels that are either hollow or come with metal gun barrels that are tubes. Older kits may need to have the barrel drilled out and I have a selection of drill bits and pin vices to hold them. I do use drill bits quite often for other jobs, so it is worth keeping a selection of micro-drill bits. Sizes from 0.3mm to 2.0mm should cover most jobs.

find sanding sticks are all I need. For metal parts, white metal or brass, then a metal file is the best tool and a fine round rat-tail file is useful for opening up holes in metal or plastic.

One issue that aircraft modellers often come across – but is also relevant to vehicle modellers – is a seam line where two large parts (often the fuselage for aircraft) do not quite meet properly and leave a small gap or a lip. Filling the gap

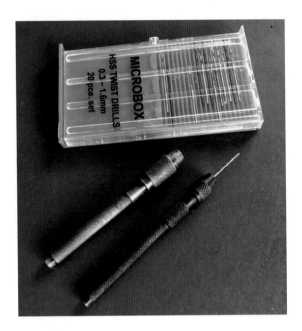

Drill bits and pin vices into which they fit come in a variety of sizes. The box shown holds drills from 0.3 to 1.6 mm in diameter.

MAKING TRACKS

Perhaps the most difficult aspect of building a model tank correctly is the tracks – particularly when it comes to small-scale models. Model tracks are available in five main forms, provided by either the kit manufacturer or as an after-market detailing set. In small scale, the most prolific are the soft vinyl-type plastic that are often referred to as 'rubber bands' – mainly because when they are put together that is what they resemble. They come in a variety of materials. The softest, almost rubber-like ones are best avoided – they have no detail, do not hold paint and do not sit properly on the suspension. The best flexible plastic tracks require only a small amount of work to make them look acceptable. The difficult part is to get them to sit correctly around drive sprockets and idlers and to look right either side of these. Similar to these but more sophisticated are the tracks from Dragon made in a patent material that they call 'DS'. This material holds crisp detail and with a little attention can be made to follow the contours of the drive sprocket and idler wheels. I have these in a separate class, as they are much better than the 'rubber bands' from other kit manufacturers. The next group are individual track links made in hard plastic. These can be challenging to make but when they are well fitted they do look good. The final type is link and length. As the name suggests, these are a mix of individual links and lengths of track links. The individual links go around drive sprockets and idlers and the lengths of track links go along the top and bottom of the suspension units. This type of track looks the best out of all the types. The final category is after-market tracks made in a semi-hard material from OKB Grigorov. These come in set lengths and by heating in hot water they can be made to bend around sprockets and idlers. Although quite expensive, they are probably the best type of tracks to use as replacements for the rubber band tracks of some small-scale models.

(continued)

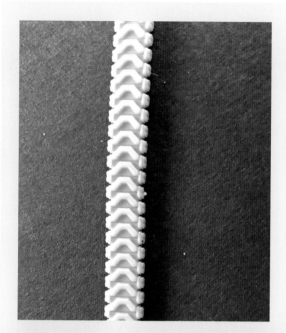

Dragon produce their small-scale tracks in a patented material they call DS. It is more detailed than older 'rubber band' tracks from other manufacturers, but needs some work to make them sit as well as link and length tracks do.

Tracks from OKB Grigorov in 1/48 scale used to replace the Hobby Boss 'rubber band' tracks. They produce a number of different track types and each pack contains several lengths of track. The spares can be used to represent additional armour, which crews sometimes welded to the front of their tanks.

Chapter 4

Painting the Model

INTRODUCTION

At every stage of creating a model, the model-maker has a chance to show artistic flair. Building the kit might involve adding some detailing parts or using parts from one kit to enhance another. However, it is the painting stage when the results of the modelmaker's artistic skills are most obvious. To some modellers this is the most daunting stage, but to many it is the most rewarding. The past ten years or so have seen a revolution in painting model vehicles. Long gone are the days of painting something a block of colour and calling it finished. Colour modulation, primers, base colours, filters, washes, weathering powders, streaking, highlights, shadows, pin washes, mud, oil stains and chipping are now all part of the vocabulary of painting and finishing a model for most. At first sight the proliferation of products

and techniques can seem daunting, but as with many things in modelmaking, practice and a willingness to experiment are the keys.

When I first started modelmaking there was little choice as to which paint to use, with only enamel paints from a small number of manufacturers readily available. Acrylic paints from a number of manufacturers are now also available. Typical of these are Vallejo, who released their first acrylic paints for modelmakers in 1992. Since the 1990s acrylics have come to dominate the modelmaking world. However, one thing that has not changed, when it comes to painting and finishing a model, is that there is no magical formula to ensure that every model you paint is perfect. But this is part of the fun. On various social media, I often read of modelmakers complaining that they cannot meet the high standards that others achieve despite slavishly applying all the techniques they have read

This 1/76 scale US Marine LVT-4 was converted from the Airfix Buffalo. I was pleased with the model ten years ago, but the awful tracks and poor dry brushing need attention!

OLIVE DRAB

Probably the most often-debated subject in model-making magazines, books and on internet forums revolves around the exact shade of what is termed 'olive drab'. The answer should be simple – but of course it is not! The origins of olive drab go back to before World War I, as a simple mix of black and ochre. Steven Zaloga in his article 'Olive drab: from the archives' relates that on 12 October 1940 the Quartermaster Corps issued orders for all material in production to be painted in Color 22 from Color Card Supplement to US Army Specification No 3–1, thereby ensuring that all vehicles leaving US armaments factories were painted to a consistent shade. Modelmakers can buy paint chips that authentically replicate these factory colours and books and magazines often have colour illustrations showing the exact shade. But is that shade appropriate for you to use on your model?

I wrote an article sometime ago about painting AFVs and entitled it: 'Fifty shades of olive drab'. Whilst this is probably an over-estimate of the number of shades of that particular colour that are available, it does reflect that manufacturers of paint for model-makers produce a bewildering number of hues of a single colour. So which is the most authentic colour available that the modeller should use? Some are certainly closer to the original factory colour than others, but there are many factors that affect how that colour actually appears when on a model. A factory-fresh vehicle will probably be a darker shade than a vehicle that has been in the field. This is due to fading in sunlight and the effects of the weather on the paint. Whilst US Army front-line units were not issued with paint, some tanks may have been painted and repainted in the field by ordnance battalions when the AFV was undergoing depot maintenance. This would inevitably lead to some variations in colour of vehicles, even in the same battalion.

There is also 'scale effect' to consider. This is a phenomenon whereby an object looks a lighter shade the further away you are from the object. Scale models look to replicate the real thing, but

A collection of paints from various manufacturers, each claiming to be olive drab or a shade thereof.

even close up will they will appear to be at a distance and so the smaller the scale the lighter the colour should be. In addition to all this the outdoor lighting conditions, from full sun or grey overcast skies, will have a major impact on the colour that the observer perceives. This leads to the question: 'is there any point in buying a paint that the manufacturer has chosen to call "olive drab"?'. All good manufacturers of paint for models will base their colours on a narrow spectrum of colours, so they are a good starting-point for the base colour.

As part of the painting process that base colour will be lightened or made darker as you go through each stage. The application of filters and washes will inevitably change the shade and once complete your model will look a different shade of olive drab to the base colour you used at the start of the painting process. So, unless you are replicating a tank as it appeared rolling off the production line, this variation is a good thing.

In summary, out of all of this mayhem about colour matching, the rule I apply is that the base colour can be accurately replicated, but the effects of weather, repainting in the field and the scale effect (as well as ambient lighting conditions) will all affect the shade you see.

about. But that is possibly the problem. Painting and finishing a model is not a competition – it is a journey. I look at some of my models from even a couple of years ago and know that my standard has improved with practice and, similarly, that in a couple of years I may look at the models I am happy with now and realize that I have improved further.

PAINT BRUSH OR AIRBRUSH?

The most expensive tool most modellers will ever buy is an airbrush and the associated air supply in the form of a compressor. Costs vary, but the airbrush will be around £100–£200 and the compressor around £150–£300. This is a major investment, so some modelmakers will choose instead to paint their models by hand. However, the paint you apply with an airbrush is much thinner than you need using a normal paint brush. This means that the fine detail is not masked and appears crisper when you use an airbrush compared to hand painting. Also, with an airbrush you can build up thin layers of paint and produce subtle shading. Therefore, for some weathering techniques or if applying a soft-edge camouflage scheme, an airbrush is essential.

For an entry level device you could buy a really cheap airbrush (around £20) and a can of compressed air (£10) and this will give you a taste of what an airbrush can do. However, a budget brush is limited in terms of the results that can

be achieved and a can of air runs out of pressure after a short time, which will inevitably interrupt a spraying session. This budget level does give you an idea of what can be achieved but can be as frustrating as it is rewarding. Cans of compressed air are cheap, compared to the outlay of buying a compressor, but if you paint many models in a year, buying cans of air can be a false economy.

Most compressors come complete with a pressure gauge, so you set the pressure of the air that flows through the airbrush. The higher the pressure the more paint will be picked up and putting too much paint defeats the object of using an airbrush. It is much better to apply several thin coats of paint rather than one thick coat, so (and this depends on the paint) I find the best pressure is around 20–40psi – but this does depend on the viscosity of the paint and this may need to be altered depending on the effect you are aiming for. To find the pressure range, spray with the paint release at maximum (trigger fully back) and then turn down the pressure until the paint stops flowing. This setting is just below the minimum.

An air compressor and can of compressed air. Cans of air can work out as a false economy if you paint more than just a few models in a year.

Vallejo Model Air paints are mixed to just the right consistency for spraying with an airbrush. Unlike some other acrylic paints they do not need to be diluted for spraying.

Increase the pressure until the paint flows with the paint release at minimum (trigger just off closed). The pressure you use should be between these two points and will vary with each different paint you use, depending on viscosity.

Some paints are 'airbrush ready' and can be used straight from the bottle. However, most paints will need to be diluted with thinners. A good rule of thumb is that the paint needs to be the consistency of single cream to get a good flow – but it is really a case of trial and error. If the paint is too thick, the airbrush will clog up and stop working; if too thin, the paint will run off the model. With the correct pressure and the paint a suitable consistency you are ready to go.

Even if you have an airbrush you will still need some paint brushes and it is essential to invest in the best you can afford. Cheap brushes are a false investment. Whilst they may seem expensive, if properly looked after good-quality brushes will last much longer than cheap brushes. The thing to look for is that a brush has a fine point. Cheap brushes will soon lose this attribute. More importantly, a cheap brush will never let you achieve the same level of detail as a more expensive one. Look after your paint brushes and they will seldom disappoint.

FACE MASKS

Using an airbrush or a spray can will produce a fine mist of paint and, whilst most of this will go onto the model, it is inevitable that some of the paint will end up in the air that you breathe in. Regardless of the paint you use, breathing in paint is dangerous and should be avoided at all costs. It is important to work in a well-ventilated area, but even more importantly a good-quality face mask is essential. A spray booth will help, but even with one of these a face mask gives you an extra layer of protection that is vital. I have used good-quality paper masks, but for full protection a half-face mask with filters is the best choice by far. A face mask is also needed when cutting or sanding resin.

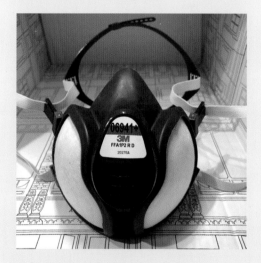

A face mask with air filters may seem like overkill, but the fine mist produced by an airbrush can be a serious health hazard.

ACRYLIC OR ENAMEL?

In the 1980s there was little choice as to which paint to use for painting military models, as only enamel paints, from a small number of manufacturers, were readily available. Since the late 1990s acrylic paints have become more popular than

Enamel paints from Humbrol. These 14ml 'tinlets' have been the single-colour traditional container for enamel paint for several decades.

Acrylic paints have been around since the 1940s as an artist medium. They have been widely available for modelmakers since the 1990s and are now more popular than enamels.

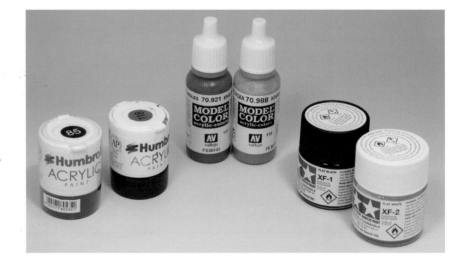

enamels and today they are the medium preferred by many modelmakers. Acrylics' main advantage is that they dry quickly, so you can apply several layers in a single modelling session. The other major advantage is that they are water based and cleaning brushes and airbrushes with water is simple and inexpensive. You can buy airbrush cleaning solutions that will give the airbrush a thorough clean and I strip my airbrush down and clean the parts after every session. Using a good cleaning solution means it only takes a few minutes and ensures the airbrush is always ready for your next session.

Enamels dry more slowly than acrylics, but some believe they give a better coverage and better definition when spraying camouflage patterns. For many years I sprayed Humbrol enamels, but recently I have moved on to acrylics, as I believe these modern paints give a coverage equal to, and sometimes better than, enamels. Tamiya Xtra Color acrylics are very easy to spray, as are the paints in the 'Model Air' range from Vallejo. I still use enamels, but mainly for painting small details like vehicle tools and stowage.

READY-MADE OR HOME-MADE?

The art of painting military vehicles has undergone something of a revolution in the recent past. New techniques of colour modulation abound, both on various websites and in printed media. Leading the charge is the very talented Mig Jimenez. The AMMO range of products is well known and some of these products feature in this book. AMMO produces the 'WWII American ETO Solution Box'. This contains all the paint and weathering products that you will need to complete models of US armour in the later stages of World War II in Europe. This book and all similar step-by-step guides can at best only be a starting-point, as any artistic pursuit (and painting model tanks is certainly that) requires skills that can be learnt to an extent through experience and practice, as well as, of course, flair and talent. The AMMO products are excellent, but there are also other products available that give equally good results. I sometimes use oil paint for washes and highlights and cheap sets of oil paints are readily available. Pastels can be used instead of pigments and mixing oil paint, enamel and varnish makes a reasonable engine oil residue. The convenience of ready-made products is of course attractive, but part of the fun of modelling is experimenting and you may find it worthwhile making your own.

The How to Paint WWII USA ETO Vehicles *book by Mig Jimenez is a good guide for painting US Army vehicles from World War II.*

Painting and your choice of paint is very subjective and as with many aspects of the hobby it can be a voyage of discovery, as you find which paint best suits you.

STEP-BY-STEP PAINTING TECHNIQUES

The rest of this chapter demonstrates the step-by-step process that I use. Alternative techniques as well as different paints and products are included. There are five basic steps that many military modelmakers follow:

1. Primer Coat. This gives a foundation for all other coats and evens out any disparities when using multi-media models.

2. Base Coat. This is a block of a single colour.

3. Shadows and highlights. These emphasize dark and light areas and include pin washes.

4. Weathering. This replicates the effects of time and weather on a vehicle.

5. Other effects. There are many other effects you can apply, such as oil stains, rusting and chips.

There are numerous guides available either in books like this one, in magazines or online as video footage. This is only a guide as to how I paint many of my models and you might decide to miss out a stage or use a different technique at a particular stage – depending on the effect you are looking to produce. Painting and weathering involves a fine balancing act to achieve the right impact. Some stages below will make your model look stark and toy-like, but these are normally followed by a stage that tones down that appearance. This may mean that you have to go back and repeat a stage. Like most things in modelmaking – but particularly in the painting stage – it is all about experimenting and trying different things. So please use the following as a basis that you can put your own spin on until you get the results you want.

Primer

The primer coat gives a key to which the following coats can adhere. For models that are built from multi-media parts (plastic, resins and etched brass) it ensures the whole model is the same colour. The primer coat also makes apparent any blemishes or holes that are not so obvious when the model is unpainted. These can be addressed and then a second coat of primer applied. Colour of primer will be decided by the final colour of the model. Some modellers use spray cans intended for spraying cars or specialist spray cans for modelmakers. For green I use a black primer and for lighter or sandy colours grey primer is best. The airbrush is set to 20–30psi and sprayed 10cm away from the model. Products to use include MIG 2023 One Shot Primer or Tamiya XF-1 Flat Black. (Vallejo #608 US olive drab primer gives a shade close to the base colour and details of a different technique for painting with an olive drab primer are given in the section about the T31 Demolition Tank.)

The primer coat is perhaps the most important of all, as this coat gives a foundation on which to build. As with all painting it is essential to apply a couple of thin layers rather than one thick one.

The 1/56-scale T31 Demolition Tank was painted following a scheme set out by Vallejo. Their primer is olive drab rather than black, as shadows in deep recesses are produced with darker shades rather than relying on the black primer showing through.

Base colour

This coat is the most important, as all the other colours will have this shade as the foundation. This base colour should be applied as thin layers and you should aim to let the black primer coat show through in the most recessed areas, as this gives a variation in colour that we will enhance as we progress. Set the airbrush to around 20–30psi at spray from about 10–15cm. Products to use include MIG 926 Olive drab base or Vallejo Model Air #043 Olive drab, or my particular favourite, Tamiya XF-62 Olive drab.

The base coat is a solid block of colour that is the most dominant shade. It will be subtly altered through the application of filters, washes and, to an extent, varnish.

Highlights

Using a fine spray from the airbrush the focus is on the areas that are most prominent – so, the top edges of hull and turret and the top edge of the turret mantlet. Airbrush is set to 10–15psi and sprayed at around 5–10cm from the model. Products to use include MIG 928 Olive drab Highlights or Vallejo #044 Light Grey Green or Tamiya XF-62 Olive drab with a little XF-57 Buff added.

Camouflage

At this stage the camouflage colour should be added. Airbrush is set to around 20psi and sprayed 5–10cm from the model. Products to use include

Highlights are applied to the surfaces that are most prominent and so would catch the sunlight. The effect is subtle and breaks up the block colour of the base coat.

Camouflage painting adds different colours to the base paint. US Army vehicles tended to be just olive drab in colour, but for Operation Cobra many units added black stripes, as shown here.

Tamiya XF-1 Flat Black or Humbrol 33 Black. (There is more information on camouflage schemes later in the book.)

Varnish layer 1

A thin layer of matt varnish at this stage will protect the work completed so far. Airbrush is set to 20–30psi and sprayed from around 10cm. Products to use include Humbrol 49 Matt Varnish. (I have used Johnsons Klear at this point. This is a floor polish that is very thin and dries to a fine

With the base coat and camouflage paint dry, I sprayed the model with a matt varnish. Some modelmakers use a gloss varnish – especially if a lot of decals are being added. The gloss sheen is then reduced through coating the model with filters and washes.

Use of a setting solution ensures that the decal adheres more effectively to the surface of the model by softening the decal. It is essential if the decal has to adhere to a rough or uneven surface.

Generally decals have a narrow overlap of clear material that can result in 'silvering' where the edge of the decal has a glossy sheen. Cutting to the exact edge of the shape gets rid of this. This is easy to do on a straight-sided decal, but not so easy on a curved shape or number.

sheen. The next stages of weathering will reduce this sheen but you may need to give the model a final thin coat of matt varnish to take away the sheen if it looks wrong.)

Application of decals (transfers)

The next stage is to apply the markings. If the area where the decal is to be fixed has an uneven surface, then a thin coat of gloss varnish will help the decal adhere to the model. Cut around the decal as close as you can and then dip in some clean warm water. Flood the area with a decal softener like Micro-soft and then after wetting the decal, place as required. Leave the decal for a couple of minutes and then once you are happy it is in the right place, dab off the excess water with a tissue or kitchen roll. Once the decal is fixed, matt varnish can be applied to bring the area around the decal to combat any silvering and bring everything back to a matt finish.

Filters

The work so far has focused on breaking up the single block of colour by adding depth and highlights, so this stage of colour modulation can seem counter-intuitive, but the idea of a filter is to blend all the colours and the markings to give them a more subtle look. Application is by a soft broad brush. Products to use include MIG 1508 Green for Grey Green.

Applying a filter by using a large brush serves to tone down the paint on the model. The photograph shows the filter being applied. When it is wet the filter has a glossy sheen which will disappear as the filter dries.

Tools and stowage

This next stage paints and fits tools and stowage to the AFV. Some kits have embossed tools fitted and whilst with smaller-scale kits this is not a problem, with the larger-scale kits they often do not look right and can be difficult to paint. I normally add spades, picks and hammers as separate items. You can buy after-market stowage items, but I sometimes make my own sheets and tarpaulins from 80g paper that has been painted with acrylics. These sheets then go over lumps of scrap plastic to depict loads. Jerry cans, blanket rolls and other stowage are then added. Tools and stowage are then covered in an appropriate wash to blend them in with the rest of the vehicle and thin thread used to depict ropes used to hold down the load.

Pin washes

Washes are used to emphasize depth. Heavily diluted paint or a specific wash is used to flow into recesses to give a false shadow that emphasizes these recesses. A pin wash focuses on raised details such as hinges and hatch covers to give them depth. Apply the pin wash with a fine point-tipped small (size 0) paint brush so you can get into recesses. (You can enhance the effect by wetting the area of interest with some thinners and then allowing the wash to run into the recesses.) If you

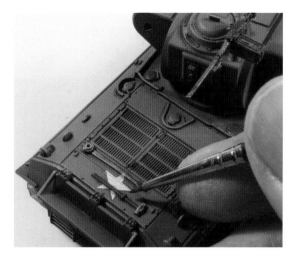

A pin wash involves applying a tiny amount of thin paint (normally a heavily diluted oil paint or enamel) to a prominent feature – in this case a tool. The paint flows around the object by capillary action to give an artificial shadow around the object.

apply too much wash then use a wide brush damp with thinners to dilute the extra paint. Products to use are MIG 1008 Dark Wash or Vallejo 76.520 Dark Khaki Green or Humbrol Dark Brown Wash Enamel. Alternatively you can heavily dilute some burnt umber oil paint (ratio 5 per cent paint to 95 per cent solvent) to make your own washes.

Fine highlighting

For this stage a small amount of oil paint is applied to the most prominent edges of the model to enhance the three-dimensional appearance. (Squeeze the oil paint onto a piece of card so that any excess linseed oil is absorbed to avoid the paint having a glossy hue.) Give the oil paint a few minutes to partially dry and then with a broad brush dipped in thinners drag the paint away from the prominent edge to give a subtle highlight. You may have to remove excess paint and then repeat to get the subtle effect required. Oil paint will dry slowly, so you will need to leave the model for a few days to totally dry out. Another method used to produce highlights is dry brushing. A small amount of enamel paint (the colour should be a very light version of the base colour) is picked up

Most of the tools shown here are provided in the kit. The stowage is separate and is shown held down by ropes, which is replicated using thin cotton.

Fine highlighting is completed by adding a fine, thin line along a prominent edge. It has to be subtly done as here, on the edge of the Sherman glacis plate.

on a medium-sized brush (size 3). Then most of the paint is brushed off onto a tissue or piece of kitchen roll. The tiny amount of paint remaining on the brush is then deposited by dragging the brush over the prominent features, such as peri-scopes and hatch covers.

Tracks

On a tracked vehicle, finding the right colour for the tracks depends on the conditions you are depicting. Even travelling only a short distance, the tracks will pick up the colour from the local terrain. I tend to paint the tracks a bright, metallic dark grey and then once dry apply a dark wash to tone everything down. Where the tracks rub on the drive sprockets I paint the tips of the teeth silver to replicate the paint being worn away.

Tracks are painted in a silver-grey paint that is then given a heavy wash of diluted oil or enamel paint.

Streaking

This technique depicts the effect of rain running down a vertical surface and dragging dust behind in subtle lines. Use a suitably fine (size 0) brush to drag streaks of burnt umber oil paint or similar down the vertical or sloped surfaces. Then using a broad, chisel-ended brush dipped in thinners, drag the oil streaks from top to bottom to create a subtle effect. Products that can be used include MIG 3513 Star-ship Filth (I love the names MIG use!) with MIG 2018 Enamel Thinner.

Chipping

Any vehicle that operates on a battlefield will be routinely subject to dents and scratches through normal use. Enemy action can result in gouges

Streaking depicts the effect of rain water dragging dust down the sides of an AFV. Lines of oil paint are applied with a thin brush to all vertical surfaces.

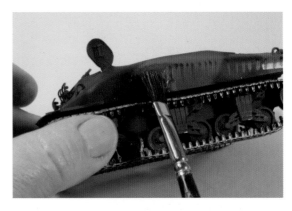

The oil paint is allowed to dry and then a broad paint brush damp with thinners is dragged down the sides of the tank. Faint but discernible lines should be left behind.

Scratches are applied using a pencil. The graphite replicates metal exposed when the paint is scratched off. Overdoing this stage can look unrealistic.

and scratches to the surface paint (or worse). This is another subtle effect that can be easily overdone and the adage 'more is less' is appropriate here. The easiest way to replicate chips is with a sharp soft pencil (2B).

Rust

Like chipping, rust is an effect that can easily be overdone. Scratches and gouges down to bare metal could rust, but are only evident as small traces. Tracks will quickly rust, but because they are constantly moving any rust will quickly flake off. The exception is tracks that are welded to a vehicle

Unpainted or untreated metal surfaces will quickly rust. Because tracks are constantly moving, any rust is quickly rubbed off. However, where tracks are welded to give additional protection, they will have a fine coat of rust.

to provide extra protection. Surface rust can be replicated with an orange and brown oil paint. Dots of the paint are applied and then dragged along the surface of the track with a broad brush dipped in thinners. A heavily damaged or wrecked vehicle if left unattended will quickly turn to rust and this can make a challenging and interesting model.

Fuel spills

Refuelling a vehicle in the field could be a hazardous business and fuel spills around refuelling points were inevitable. Many US tanks have raised metal crescents around refuelling caps to catch spilt fuel. Stains can be replicated using a black enamel mixed with burnt umber oil paint with a gloss varnish (for example, Humbrol 35) in the area around the fuel cap. A small amount of this can be streaked down a vertical surface using a brush loaded with thinners.

Varnish layer 2

A thin layer of matt varnish at this stage will protect the work before going on to weather the model. It is not always necessary and depends on how much final weathering you intend to apply in the next stages. Set the airbrush set to around 10–20psi and spray from around 10cm. Products to use include MIG 2056 Satin Lucky Varnish or Vallejo #522 Satin Varnish or Humbrol 49 Matt Varnish.

During refuelling it is almost inevitable that some fuel will be spilt. US tanks often had a small bund around the fuel caps to catch any spills.

The AFV is given a coat of matt varnish to protect the paint from the effects of the weathering process. The weathering solutions can be aggressive and react with the coats of paint, so a barrier is essential. The varnish can be applied at an earlier stage if desired.

Pigments have been applied to the tracks and suspension of this Sherman. If the tank is not going to be handled much this pigment layer can be left, but a pigment fixer should be used if the model is going to be handled a lot.

WEATHERING YOUR MODEL

So far we have looked at the AFV above the suspension. The tracks and suspension of a vehicle will bear the brunt of driving through muddy or dusty environments and so this is the area we will concentrate on next. Although the techniques below concentrate on the suspension, dust and mud will be present on the whole AFV and that should be borne in mind when applying these methods.

Dust

Having to operate in dusty conditions can occur in a variety of climates. US forces were engaged in hot countries such as Tunisia and had to cope with the equatorial conditions in the Pacific, often on sandy or volcanic beaches. Dry, arid conditions were prevalent in Sicily and Italy and, in the summer of 1944, dry and dusty conditions were prevalent throughout northwest Europe.

Modelling pigments are a relatively new material that can be used to effectively replicate dust, as they have a similar consistency to the real thing. Applied with a medium brush (size 4) the pigments are brushed into the tracks and suspension.

If too much has accumulated you can remove with the brush and, once you are happy, spray the dust with thinners or pigment fixer with the airbrush set to low pressure (10psi). For the turret and upper hull a thin coating of pigment can be brushed on, and then by drawing a brush damp with thinners down the sides of the hull and turret (very much as for streaking above) you can replicate the effect of rain streaks in the dust.

Applying the right amount of pigment in order for it to look realistic can be challenging and I am not a great fan of pigments. Another way to replicate dust is to spray the AFV with suitable enamel paint such as Humbrol 74 Linen, Humbrol 83 Ochre or Humbrol 121 Pale Stone – depending on the effect you are looking to replicate. The airbrush should be set low (10psi) to give a very fine mist – almost like a filter – but concentrating on the suspension and tracks or wheels. Before the paint dries, load a medium, chisel-ended brush with thinners and drag this over the whole model, allowing the thinned paint to collect in crevices and around details. Once dry the dust will be left to give a subtle effect.

Whether using pigments or enamels or even a combination of the two, the overall effect of dusting might be that some of the detail revealed at

Crews would work hard to keep tracks and suspension free of mud, as a build up of mud could cause the tank to throw a track or worse. So the application of mud in model form should be kept to a minimum. There are of course exceptions to this rule!

stage 8 (pin washes) is lost and so you may need to re-apply a pin wash to some places at this stage.

Mud

There are many photographs of US armour bogged down in mud – particularly in Italy and in the Battle of the Bulge in late 1944 to early 1945. Tank tracks are particularly good at churning up wet earth. Crews will try to keep tracks clear, as compacted mud can cause tracks to snap or just stop running. This is not always possible, but when modelling a muddy scene it is worth bearing in mind that tracks are designed to throw off mud and so – unless you are modelling a bogged-down vehicle – any coating of mud on your model should be thin.

As with the above description for dust, pigments can be used to replicate mud – but apply a much thicker coat. Alternatively you can buy pots of ready-made 'mud', such as AK Interactive AK 016 Fresh Mud or Vallejo 73.801 European Splash Mud. Like pigments they are applied by brush, but do not require fixing. Another alternative is to mix plaster and water-based paint to make a thick 'glop' that can be applied as appropriate.

PAINTING SMALL-SCALE MODELS

Some of the techniques above can be applied to small-scale models. However, in the smaller scales the subtle effects can be difficult to reproduce. So the following processes are a truncated version of the stages shown above. There is a separate set of techniques for wargamers; the emphasis is on producing large numbers in a short time. Painting time is kept down to a minimum in this section and I demonstrate techniques that rely on hand painting and aerosol cans rather than airbrush spray painting.

Model collectors

Primer

The primer coat is the most important coat, as it gives a key to which the following coats can adhere. Once a thin coat of primer has been applied any defects, such as blemishes or holes, become more apparent and can be rectified. Primer coats must be thin – particularly on small-scale models, as fine details are easily obscured with thick paint layers. An airbrush is ideal but a spray can will do the job. For US olive drab tanks I use a black primer, but for lighter-coloured tanks (desert yellow) a grey primer should be used. The dark primer showing through the later coats can help emphasize the shadows in smaller-scale models. If using an airbrush, then MIG 2005 Black Primer is ideal.

Base colour

This coat is the foundation. This base colour should be applied as thin layers with the airbrush set to around 10–20psi with spraying at around 10cm. Products to use include MIG 925 Olive drab Dark Base or Vallejo Model Air #013 Olive Yellow or Tamiya XF-61 Dark Green.

Like the 1/48-scale models, this 1/72 Mine Roller tank has been given a black primer coat.

A base coat of olive drab has been sprayed over the primer coat on this M4A1.

Lighter coat

The base coat covers the whole model. This second coat is a lighter shade than the base and the emphasis is on the more prominent surfaces of the model. These are the surfaces that would catch the light the most on the real vehicle and this paint is applied sparingly and not over the whole model. The airbrush is set to 10–15psi. Paint suitable for this coat includes MIG 927 Olive drab Light or Vallejo Model Air #043 or Tamiya XF-62 Olive drab.

Camouflage

At this stage any camouflage colour you are using should be added. The airbrush is set to around 15–20psi and sprayed 5–10cm from the model.

A lighter highlight coat has been applied to the prominent edges of this 1/72-scale M4 Medium Tank.

A camouflage of black paint has been applied to this 1/72-scale Sherman. The paint was sprayed on from an airbrush to give a soft edge. A hard edge can be applied using a broad paint brush.

Not all US Army tanks were painted in olive drab. This M4A1 Medium Tank depicts a tank used in Sicily and has an olive drab and ochre camouflage scheme applied with an airbrush.

Products for an Olive Green and Black pattern include Tamiya XF-1 Flat Black or Humbrol 33 Black. Sand colours such as MIG 138 Desert Yellow can be used for tanks that were used in warmer climes like the Mediterranean or Pacific theatres.

Varnish layer

A thin layer of varnish at this stage will protect the work completed so far. Gloss varnish can be applied as the following stages will reduce the sheen that a gloss varnish produces. The advantage of a gloss varnish is that it ensures the decals adhere to the surface of the model, but if you

A thin layer of varnish has been applied to protect the paint from the next stages.

A green filter has been applied all over this tank using a broad brush.

are not going to go much further with filters and weathering then a matt varnish is best. The airbrush is set to 20psi and sprayed from around 10cm. Products to use include MIG 2056 Satin Lucky Varnish or Vallejo #522 Satin Varnish or Humbrol 49 Matt Varnish.

Application of decals (transfers)

Cut around the decal as close as you can as some decals exhibit 'silvering', which is an unrealistic sheen around the marking. Dip the decal into some clean warm water, then apply some decal softener like Micro-Set to the model and then place the decal as required. Leave the decal for ten minutes and then dab off the excess water with a kitchen roll. Leave the decal to set and then apply matt varnish over the decal to bring everything back to a matt finish.

Filters

The model is now close to completion, but it can have a toy-like appearance at this stage. If the colours look subtly blended then you can skip this stage, but if the appearance is garish with obvious borders between shades then a filter will blend everything in to make the shades more subtle. A filter is a heavily-diluted wash of the base colour. Application is by a soft broad brush all over the model. You can make your own filter by diluting a base shade or a product like MIG 1508 Green for Grey Green is suitable.

Tools and stowage

Small-scale models often have tools already moulded to the tank. For a more realistic model you can scrape off these tools and add separate items. A few kits come with stowage and you can buy after-market stowage items, although I make my own sheets and tarpaulins from thin paper that has been painted with acrylics as shown above. Separate tools and stowage are painted off the tank and then fitted as appropriate.

Pin washes

There is a difference between washes and filters. Filters seek to blend in colours, but washes are used to emphasize depth and a pin wash focuses on prominent details to replicate this depth. A pin

Tools and stowage have been added here. A thin wash emphasizes the shadows on the tied-down stowed kit.

The effect of the pin wash is particularly noticeable here. The paint has flowed neatly around the cupola and the other prominent features on the turret roof of this US Marine Corps Sherman.

Brown and white oil paint has been applied to the hull and turret as the first stage in the streaking process.

wash is applied with a fine brush around items such as hatches and periscopes. Commercial products like MIG 1008 Dark Wash or Vallejo 76.520 Dark Khaki Green or Humbrol Dark Brown Wash Enamel are suitable. A home-made wash of heavily diluted Burnt Umber oil paint (ratio 5 per cent paint to 95 per cent solvent) can be used to make your own washes.

Tracks

I normally paint the tracks a bright, metallic dark grey and then, once dry, apply a dark wash over all the tracks to tone everything down. 'Rubber band' tracks should be painted separately from the model and then fitted. Where the tracks come as part of the suspension, or if you have used link and length tracks, then you will need to paint these as part of the main model.

Streaking

This stage depicts the effect of rain running down a vertical surface producing subtle streaks of dust. A fine (size 0) brush is used to drag streaks of burnt umber and white oil paint or MIG 1203 Streaking Grime down the vertical surfaces of the model. Leave the paint for a few minutes to partially dry (it would take several hours or even days to fully dry), and then drag a broad, chisel-ended brush that

A broad brush dipped in thinners has been dragged along the hull and turret sides to produce the effect seen here.

has been dipped in thinners along the oil streaks from top to bottom.

Chipping, rust and fuel spills

Other details can now all be added as set out above. However, I find that in the smaller scale these effects are either so subtle that they become invisible at a normal viewing range or are overdone to the extent that they look unrealistic.

Weathering

This stage involves the application of pigments to replicate dust. These are liberally applied to horizontal surfaces with a broad brush. Mixing colours of pigment can produce subtle colour changes.

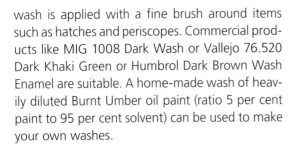

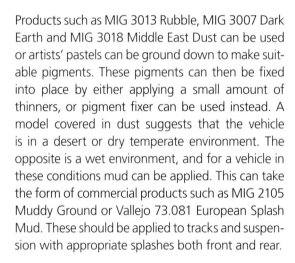

Pigments have been used on the suspension units, track and horizontal surfaces to depict a tank in a dry dusty environment.

The prominent edges of this tank have been dry brushed to emphasize highlights.

Products such as MIG 3013 Rubble, MIG 3007 Dark Earth and MIG 3018 Middle East Dust can be used or artists' pastels can be ground down to make suitable pigments. These pigments can then be fixed into place by either applying a small amount of thinners, or pigment fixer can be used instead. A model covered in dust suggests that the vehicle is in a desert or dry temperate environment. The opposite is a wet environment, and for a vehicle in these conditions mud can be applied. This can take the form of commercial products such as MIG 2105 Muddy Ground or Vallejo 73.081 European Splash Mud. These should be applied to tracks and suspension with appropriate splashes both front and rear.

Dry brushing
This stage highlights the prominent features. Although I generally do this as the last stage, it can also be undertaken before applying filters and washes. I tend to apply it last as it really emphasizes the detail, but I accept that some would see this as an over-emphasis and not realistic. A small amount of enamel paint (I use Humbrol Matt 83 to highlight Olive drab) is picked up on a broad brush (size 2) and the paint is lightly rubbed on some kitchen roll so that the brush is almost dry. Gently rub this brush over the model so that most of the paint is deposited on the highlighted parts of the model (periscopes, hull edges and hatch details). If the paint is deposited on flat surfaces then it can be easily

removed with a separate brush dipped in thinners. As with many stages of painting model tanks, the old adage 'less is more' definitely applies here.

Varnish
A thin layer of matt varnish at this stage will protect the final work and bring everything together. The airbrush is set to about 10–20psi and sprayed at around 10cm from the model. Products to use include Humbrol 49 Matt Varnish.

MODELS FOR WARGAMERS

For most wargamers, painting and finishing models is secondary to re-enacting battles on the table top. However, many wargamers will still want a good level of detail, so this section reduces the time taken to paint your models and the models are finished by hand painting or using paint from a spray can rather than an airbrush.

Primer
This most important stage provides the foundation for all other stages. Blemishes and holes will become more apparent and can be addressed now. Some recommend car primer paint from 'rattle cans', which is suitable if applied thinly. Primer paint spray cans from model manufacturers such as Tamiya and manufacturers of paint for models

Wargamers will probably prefer to spend their money on building up an army rather than expensive things like an air brush and compressor. Models can be painted with spray cans and paint brushes to produce some good effects. A 'rattle can' black primer has been used here.

such as Humbrol can give a better finish. Black is a good primer for olive drab and a grey or white is more suitable for lighter shades.

Base coat

As indicated previously, an airbrush and compressor are probably the most expensive items that the modeller will buy. However, for wargamers or modelmakers with a limited budget, the priority will most likely be model kits and *not* an airbrush and compressor. Nevertheless, some good effects can be achieved by hand painting. For the base coat a thin layer of olive drab is applied using a brush (size 3). It is better to apply two thin coats

rather than one thick coat and suitable products are MIG 927 Olive drab Light or Vallejo Model Air #043 or Tamiya XF-62 Olive drab.

Camouflage

If you are applying a camouflage scheme, now is the time to do this. Olive drab and Black was the scheme applied to some US tanks in the European theatre for Operation *Cobra*. Campaigns in North Africa, Sicily and Italy used a variety of shades of yellow and green, and for tanks in the Pacific there are numerous unusual schemes of various shades of green, yellow and red. (*See* the different sections later in the book for more details.)

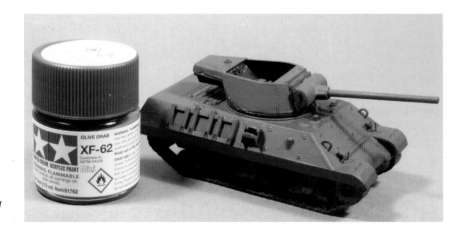

This Armourfast M36 has been hand painted. It is essential to use thin paint to avoid obscuring details.

US Marine Corps tanks often appeared in different schemes of yellow/sand, red and green. Different schemes were applied by different units.

Tools and stowage

Simple models for wargamers normally have tools embossed onto the model. Now is the time to paint these. If you are adding stowage and additional tools, these are available from various manufacturers such as Black Dog or you can make your own. These should be painted separately from the vehicle and then fixed to the tank.

Tracks

The tracks that are part of the model and the separate 'rubber band' tracks are now painted and fitted to the tank. I make my own track colour using a medium grey with some silver added, but proprietary track colours such as MIG-3008 Track Rust and MIG-3009 Gun Metal or Tamiya X-10 Gun Metal are suitable.

This stowage is from Black Dog. Made in resin it looks good and is easy to paint and fit.

PAINT AND BUILD

The traditional way to build and paint a model is to do it in that order. The model is put together and then painted. However, if the model is a simple one with a minimum number of parts, then it is possible to paint the model on the sprue and then put the kit together. Painting on the sprue means it is easy to apply an even coat and there are no hard-to-reach points as there would be on an already-constructed model. Tracks and wheels are easier to paint on the sprue and if you use a suitable shade of paint in a spray can, painting a squadron of small-scale tanks can be completed in minutes. The disadvantage comes if the fit of parts is poor and you need to apply filler or if some of the glue oozes out of a joint and is deposited on the visible surface of the vehicle. These problems can be resolved with a little touching up once the filler and glue are dry. While this is not a technique I have used personally, I can see its attraction to some wargamers, whose models often have only a minimal number of parts.

Wargames tanks like this Armourfast M36 have a minimal amount of parts that can be painted on the sprue. Once built, any areas where the paint is missing can be patched up by hand.

Washes

Once the base coat is dry the model can be given a thin coat of a suitable wash. (If you have used enamel paints, then you will need to seal these with a suitable varnish before applying an enamel-based wash.) This wash acts partially like a filter to tone down the base coat but also pools into recesses to add depth to prominent features. Suitable products include MIG 1008 Dark Wash or Vallejo 76.520 Dark Khaki Green or Humbrol Dark Brown Wash Enamel. Or you can use a home-made wash of heavily-diluted burnt umber oil paint.

Streaking

Use a fine (size 0) brush to drag streaks of burnt umber and white oil paint or MIG 1203 Streaking Grime down vertical sloped surfaces. Allow a few minutes for the paint to partially dry and then use a broad, chisel-ended brush dipped in thinners to drag the oil paint streaks from top to bottom.

Dry brushing

With the previous stages dry it is time to highlight the prominent features. Using a lighter shade of the base coat, dip a broad brush into the paint and wipe off most of the paint on a piece of kitchen roll. Brush the model, with the prominent parts of the model receiving most of the residual paint. This technique requires some practice to perfect but can look good. I use enamel paints for this stage, as the paint dries more slowly than acrylics, so you can wipe away any excess paint using a broad brush and thinners.

Varnish

Applying a thin layer of matt varnish at this stage will protect the model from handling. As with previous coats it is essential to apply a thin layer of varnish to the model. Products to use include Humbrol 49 Matt Varnish.

Weathering

For many wargamers the model is now complete. It may need putting on a suitable base to reduce the need to touch the actual model. However, some wargamers – particularly those who are wargaming in 28mm or larger scales – will want to add more by weathering to the model as shown below. Chipping, oil staining and rust can also be added at this point as required and, once all these effects are complete and dry, a final coat of matt varnish will finish the model.

Streaking along the hull and turret sides gives this wargames tank a worn look.

Light weathering and a dusting of pigment finished off this M36 tank destroyer, which is now ready for the wargames table.

Chapter 5

Dioramas and Scenic Bases

INTRODUCTION

One of the many advantages of modelling in small scale is that in the space taken up by a single 1/35 scale model it is possible to depict a scene with several small-scale vehicles.

PLINTHS AND BASES

Plinths on which to mount dioramas can be made from a variety of materials, but the most popular are wooden bases. These can either be bought from a variety of suppliers or made at home. The main factor to consider is that the wood is free of knots and will not warp. Medium Density Fibreboard (MDF) is a cheap alternative to wood. Once you have decided on your material, it is cut to the desired size and shape and then either left with a straight edge or given a shaped edge with a router. The wooden base forms a plinth, but if you want to finish your base without a plinth then a material such as acrylic perspex sheeting is ideal. I use cheap picture frames for many of my plinths. These can be bought in a variety of sizes and frames have different thicknesses. The scenery can be built directly onto the plinth, but it is easier to build everything on a suitable base and then glue that base to the plinth. Acrylic sheet or thick plastic card are ideal, as long as they are

A diorama using small-scale allied vehicles depicting a D-Day scene. This base is 70cm by 35cm and features thirteen vehicles and dozens of figures in 1/76 scale. In 1/35 scale this base would be big enough for only three or at most four vehicles.

These bases are made from solid wood and are big enough to display a single small-scale vehicle.

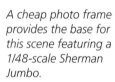

A cheap photo frame provides the base for this scene featuring a 1/48-scale Sherman Jumbo.

rigid enough to ensure they do not warp. Some of the cheaper photo frames have perspex instead of glass and these are ideal to use as a base.

SCENERY

Whilst street scenes can be flat with level roads, a natural landscape will have hills and gradients, lumps and bumps. Having scenery at different heights adds interest and enables several models to be put together in a small amount of space, as it exploits all three dimensions. Polystyrene packaging or ceiling tiles can be cut up to form the base and then covered in plaster. Alternatively, plaster-impregnated bandage will produce a suitable lumpy surface. I add a small amount of water-based muddy brown to the plaster and then if any chips off subsequently you do not end up with white patches. The terrain is then painted with a diluted water-based paint. Acrylics or poster paints from an art shop can be used as the base

These flowers are for a model railway and approximate to 1/48 scale. The base is an old cork and big enough to display a couple of figures.

basic shell and, although the walls are overly thick, detailing can be added to make these buildings more realistic. Revell 1/76-scale kits (formerly Matchbox) include a small diorama base and these are an excellent source of walls and damaged buildings that can be combined with other models to make a convincing street scene. Kits are available in resin and plastic from a variety of makers. Ruins and complete buildings in resin that depict actual buildings are available from a variety of manufacturers from Europe-based manufacturers such as DIO Dump and DIO 72. Most late World War II dioramas featuring British vehicles will be set in northwest Europe, and these buildings look very different to British buildings. One good source of buildings is from manufacturers of model continental railways. Although mostly undersized (because they are 1/87 scale) they do make realistic backgrounds. Model-railway buildings can be adapted by using some of the numerous detailing kits available both in plastic and recently introduced laser-cut wood.

colour. Grass and vegetation is then added and model railway suppliers can provide a suitable source of materials. Trees can be difficult to build, but you can buy realistic ready-made trees, but they are not cheap. For a diorama, a small tree is probably sufficient to fill a corner and they can be scratch-built, from a kit or ready-made. The garden or local park may also provide a source of twigs and roots that can be painted and used to represent fallen or war-torn trunks.

STREET SCENES

Many photographs from World War II show vehicles travelling along ruined streets and these scenes can be replicated using small-scale buildings in a variety of states of distress. Airfix and Italeri manufacture some resin and injection-moulded plastic buildings specifically for wargamers that can be adapted for dioramas. These are a good

This street scene is in 1/76 scale and uses Airfix resin buildings that have additional details added to enhance the realism.

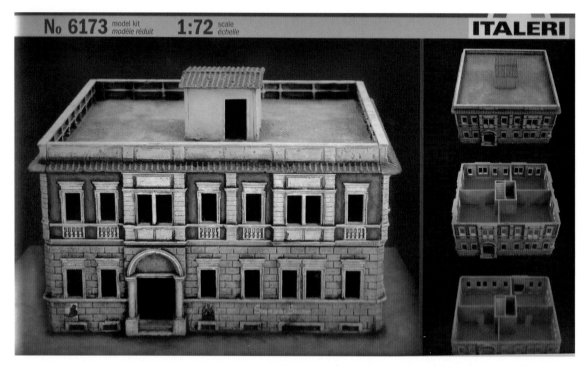

There are numerous buildings available in the Italeri range. This one depicts a Berlin building and other kits can be added to make a multiple-storey building.

Resin and plaster buildings from a number of suppliers can be used as the basis of dioramas for AFVs. The dead tree is homemade, using components provided by the appropriately named company 'Treemendus'.

This building from DioDump is made of plaster and features the Ardennes farm Yard 'Vielsalm'. The building comes complete with a small packet of realistic snow.

This is another Airfix resin building designed for wargamers with some extra rubble added to depict a ruined French café.

SAND

In small scale, normal sand does not look realistic, as a sand grain in 1/72 would be microscopic. For this reason I don't use real sand in my dioramas to depict deserts or beaches, but prefer instead to use water-based paint that has been thickened by adding fine plaster. However, not all deserts or beaches consist of fine sand. Both can be mainly rock or stones and pebbles and for that I use N-gauge railway ballast sprinkled over a wet painted surface. Depending on the effect being modelled, I then paint over the ballast with the thick paint mix. Rocks can be depicted using stones from the garden. They need to be painted and then suitably weathered and can either be rugged or smooth depending on the scene being depicted.

WATER

As with sand, real water simply does not look right on a diorama. The depth of water modelled will dictate the medium I use. For shell holes I pour a small amount of matt varnish into the hole. For deeper holes I will pour in one layer, allow it to dry and then add a few splashes of paint or flock powder before pouring in more gloss varnish. This gives the hole the appearance of more depth. Some dioramas depict landing craft or amphibious vehicles at sea. For this I use Vallejo 'Still Waters', a material that can be poured and dries crystal clear. For sea dioramas involving vehicles I add some green paint to the mixture, then I pour several thin layers over a light-green plaster base. For the last layer I add a little white enamel paint and then before this layer dries I apply the handle of an old paint brush to produce the troughs that depict the water being churned up.

Depicting a seascape can be challenging. Here an American-built DUKW in British use is depicted running alongside a ship, having picked up some stores.

Chapter 6

Light Tanks

LIGHT TANKS M3 AND M5 (STUART)

In an earlier chapter we explored the rivalry in the 1930s between the US Army, Infantry and Cavalry. This rivalry was particularly apparent when it came to light tanks. The infantry experimented with the new T2 Light Tank and, based on this AFV, the cavalry brought the M1 Combat Car into service in 1937. With the creation of the Armored Force in July 1940, the division between infantry and cavalry was finally healed and the designation of their tanks was changed to Light Tanks M1A1 and M1A2. Developments of these tanks led to the Light Tank M2 series and this in turn led to the Light Tank M3 that entered production in March 1941.

The M2A4 saw limited combat in the Pacific, but it was the M3 that would perform extensive war service – particularly with the British in the Western Desert, where the General Stuart (sometimes called 'Honey') was gratefully received, as it was as well armed and armoured as the British Crusader medium tank and far more reliable. Changes were introduced to improve the M3 as it went through production. Most significant was the move from riveted to welded turrets and hulls.

The M3A1 entered into production in June 1942. This tank had the cupola removed and a gyro stabilizer fitted to the 37mm gun; the two sponson-mounted machine guns were also removed. A radical redesign of the rear hull

The M3 and M5 Light Tanks were widely used by the US Army and Marines, but many found their way into the armouries of other allied nations. This M3A1 was photographed in a museum in Belgrade some years ago.

resulted in the M3A3, which had room for extra fuel tanks and more ammunition and entered production in early 1943. Lessons from the British experience in the Western Desert were incorporated in this model, including sand-shields.

The M3 was powered by a Continental W-670 seven-cylinder petrol engine. These were always in short supply and, to address this, the Cadillac division of GMC fitted a Cadillac Twin V8 in a standard M3. Fitting the new engine in a hull that was similar to the M3A3 resulted in a new AFV. The Light Tank M5 had a new rear hull to accommodate the new engine, a sloping glacis plate and a Cadillac Hydra-matic transmission. An M3A1 turret was fitted to the M5, but when supplies of

The M5 Light Tank was a cheap tank to build and very popular with minor nations that had a limited defence budget after World War II. This tank is in a military museum in Lisbon, Portugal.

Variant	Production	Description
M3	5,811 (1,285 Guiberson diesel)	Initially riveted hull with welded multi-faced turret. Later production cast or welded round turret with welded hull.
M3A1	4,621 (211 Guiberson diesel and a few Continental)	Cast or welded turret and welded hull with gyro stabilizer and no cupola.
M3A3	3,427	Redesigned welded hull with sloped glacis and revised turret with rear bulge to accept SCR 508 radio.
M5	2,074	Twin Cadillac engine with box-like rear engine cover and sloping glacis.
M5A1	6,810	M5 hull with M3A3 turret. Large access hatches and improved vision devices.

the much better M3A3 turret became available these were fitted to the M5 hull to produce the Light Tank M5A1. This vehicle remained in production until June 1944, when the all-new Light Tank M24 began to enter mass production.

The M3 and M5 Light Tanks series were generally used for reconnaissance and scouting. However, some were modified to carry out different roles. One of the more unusual was the M3 with Maxson Turret, which mounted a quad 0.5in cal turret in an anti-aircraft role. A single prototype was built but rejected in favour of the same mounting fitted in an M3 Half-track.

Some M3s, M3A1s and M5A1s were fitted with flame-guns and employed in the Pacific theatre. A small number of M3s and M5s were fitted as Command Tanks and some M5s had their turrets removed to produce the T8 Reconnaissance Vehicle. Attempts to make the M5 a mortar carrier went no further than a few prototypes due to the limited space within the hull. Experiments with mounting 3in and 75mm guns ceased at unsuccessful trials with the exception of the Howitzer Motor Carriage M8 that fitted a M1A1 75mm pack howitzer in a modified turret on an M5 hull (*see* Chapter 10).

LIGHT TANK (AIRBORNE) M22 (LOCUST)

In the autumn of 1941 Marmon Herrington delivered the T9 pilot model of an airborne tank. Designed to be transported either inside or underneath a suitable transport aircraft, the T9 was modified following trials to become the T9E1 and eventually the M22 Light Tank (Airborne), colloquially known as the 'Locust'. A total of 830 tanks were built but none would ever be used by US forces in anger. Within the weight limitations the M22 was well armed with a 37mm gun and armour of 25mm, comparable with the widely-used M24 Light Tank. The reason for the Locust not being used by the US Army related more to the lack of a suitable transport aircraft for it rather than limitations of the tank itself. The M22 Light Tank could be carried externally by a C54 cargo plane, but only after the turret had been removed. This posed significant tactical problems. The British had designed the Hamilcar glider to carry their own Tetarch airborne tank and they took delivery of a large number of M22s, but only a few were used in support of the Rhine crossing in March 1945.

LIGHT TANK M24 (CHAFFEE)

The British army's experience with the M3 Light Tank in the Western Desert persuaded the Americans that any future light tank should carry a heavier weapon than the 37mm fitted to the M3 and M5 Light Tanks. The 75mm M6 gun was used in the Mitchell bomber and the complex recoil system made it ideal to fit in the limited space in a light tank. The M3 and M5 Light Tanks were too small to take either the M6 gun or the larger 75mm ammunition and so the Ordnance Department tasked Cadillac with producing an all-new light tank. The M24 Light Tank weighed 18 tons, armour was a thin 25mm but the gently sloping armour, low silhouette and high speed (56km/h/35mph on roads) were envisaged as giving sufficient protection in the reconnaissance role. Trials of the first two pilot models in October 1943 were so successful that a production run of 1,000 vehicles was ordered by the Ordnance Department. This was quickly increased to 5,000 and by the end of World War II 4,415 vehicles of all types had been built. The M24 Light Tank (called Chaffee by the British) gradually replaced the M5 Light Tank from late 1944 and served with US and British tank battalions until the end of the war.

The M24 Light Tank was widely used after World War II and this example is in the Aalborg Garrison Museum in Denmark.

A close-up, detailed shot of another museum M24, showing the combined headlamp and siren brush guard.

The design of the M24 Light Tank was highly successful, as it combined speed, reliability and ruggedness with a big punch for such a small AFV. Experiments to mount the 105mm M4 Howitzer and the 155mm M1 Howitzer would result in the M37 Howitzer Motor Carriage and M41 Howitzer Motor Carriage respectively. The M19 Gun Motor Carriage carried twin 40mm on an M24 chassis

in a special turret set on the rear of the hull with the engines moved to the centre of the hull. Most M19s, M37s and M41s were delivered after World War II had ended, but they went on to serve for many years in the post-war world.

BUILDING THE M3 AND M5 SERIES OF LIGHT TANKS

M5 in 1/72 scale

Mirage US Light Tank M5 (Tunisia 1942) Kit 726077

OKB Grigorov Tracks for M3/5 Family T16E1 P72173

Models of the M3, M3A1 and M5 Light tanks are available from Revell (formerly Matchbox) and Milicast in 1/76 scale. In 1/72 scale Poland-based Mirage produce a number of US Light Tanks. Their M5 looks very realistic built straight out of the box. I added OKB Grigorov tracks to replace the soft plastic ones that come with the kit, but otherwise little needs to be done to the kit to produce an accurate replica.

These Stuart tanks in 1/76 scale were originally Matchbox models that are now available from Revell. A US M3 is in the foreground with a British 8th Army Stuart behind. This model was built straight out of the box with decals from the Matchbox kit.

The Mirage M5 Light Tank from Mirage in 1/72 scale. The only major change is the tracks from OKB Grigorov used to replace those in the kit.

M3 with Maxson Turret in 1/76 scale

Revell M3A1 Stuart 'Honey' kit 03224

Revell M16 Halftrack Kit 03228 (Quad MG turret only)

The Maxson quad 0.5in calibre anti-aircraft gun was more normally mounted on the M16 MGC. A trailer-mounted version (the M45) was introduced in 1943 and was still in use in the Vietnam war. This version is a later model, housed in a military museum in Olso, Norway.

The M3 armed with a Maxson turret in 1/76 scale is a simple conversion using the M3 Stuart and M16 Halftrack, both from Revell (formerly Matchbox). The Revell 1/76-scale M3 Light Tank first appeared under the 'Matchbox' label in 1978. The M16 was also originally from 'Matchbox' and appeared in 1974. Considering the age of the kits they have withstood the test of time and, whilst not as precise as more modern kits, they build into reasonable models and were combined here to make the intriguing M3 with Maxson turret that went no further than a single prototype.

The M3 was built straight out of the box with the only change being to replace the kit headlamps with a pair found in the spares box. The Maxson turret was improved by adding some extra detailing to the rear of the turret based on a series of photographs of the M16 Halftrack. The model was painted olive drab and lightly weathered with no markings as per the prototype.

The M3 with Maxson turret is a simple conversion using two Revell kits in 1/76 scale.

The completed M3 Maxson conversion mounted on the Revell trailer that comes with the Diamond T Tank Transporter kit.

BUILDING THE M22 LIGHT TANK (AIRBORNE)

There are three different kits of the M22 available: first, the Bronco kit is in 1/35 scale; then there are two further kits in 1/72 – a quick-fit kit with two models from S Models and a resin kit from Planet Models. Milicast Models produce an M22 in 1/76 scale as a ready-built resin model in their 'Battlefield' series. The Planet Models kit was built straight out of the box and finished in olive drab with British Airborne markings provided in the kit.

The M22 Locust in 1/72 scale. The kit from Planet Models comes with decals for the British airborne division – the only troops to use the Locust in action. The only addition made to the kit was to add the bars on the suspension.

BUILDING THE M24

> ### M24 Light Tank in 1/72 Scale
>
> OKB Grigorov 1/72 M24 Chaffee USA WWII Light Tank Kit R72001
>
> OKB Grigorov Side Skirts for M24 Chaffee P72017
>
> OKB Grigorov Detail set for M24 Chaffee P72018
>
> OKB Grigorov Turret bin for M24 Chaffee P72020
>
> OKB Grigorov Metal Barrel for M24 Chaffee S72357
>
> OKB Grigorov Resin idler wheels for M24 Chaffee

OKB Grigorov is a Bulgarian-based company that specializes in making after-market tracks and running gear for models, mainly in 1/72 and 1/48 scale with some 1/35 wheels and some 1/350-scale model tanks. They have recently branched out and produced complete kits of AFVs including an M24 Chaffee Light Tank. The kit is injection moulded and available as an 'economy' version or a 'Mammoth' version. The latter comes with

The OKB Grigorov 'Mammoth' M24 kit comes with separate etched brass kits for the side skirts and turret bin as well as a detailing set. This includes brush guards, additional parts for the HMG, as well as tiny components to add extra detail to the hull and turret. A turned-brass gun barrel is included with the kit.

the plastic kit and all of the after-market detailing parts listed above. (The kit comes in the largest box I have ever seen for a 1/72-scale kit!) Three grey plastic sprues hold the 200+ parts and the kit includes link and length tracks. Assembly was generally straightforward, but if you are adding the etched-brass parts, these need to be incorporated during construction. This is not immediately obvious as there are separate instructions for the plastic kit and the etched-brass parts.

Care needs to be taken to ensure that you do not build as per the kit instructions and then have to undo this work to replace it with the etched-brass parts. The track guards are typical of this issue, as they need some major surgery to remove the plastic supports and this inevitably means scrapping off the rivet detail, which has to be added as the final stage using small bits of plastic rod. I had to add some micro-strip to widen the track covers, as they did not extend beyond the edge of the track, meaning the side skirts did not fit. Further micro-strip was added to the etched-brass supports and along the hull edge. Filler was needed to fill the gap between the track guards and the front hull and a little filler was added to the rear chassis to fill two square holes that are not needed on the early version I depicted. The turret-mounted 0.50cal machine gun and mount were upgraded using the etched-brass set and having upgraded several 1/48 scale HMG this was relatively straightforward. The OKB Grigorov Chaffee is probably one of the best small-scale kits on the market. Adding the etched-brass parts is quite challenging

and not for junior or inexperienced modelmakers, but the effort is all worth it as the kit can be built to a standard that rivals larger-scale kits.

The completed M24 Light Tank. All of the etched brass parts and the turned-metal barrel produce an accurate version of this late war tank in 1/72 scale.

The level of detail of the completed OKB Grigorov M24 Light Tank is the most detailed Chaffee available in 1/72 scale and rivals even 1/35-scale AFVs for the amount of detail.

Chapter 7

Medium Tanks

M3 MEDIUM SERIES (GENERAL LEE)

By the outbreak of the war in Europe in September 1939, the US Ordnance Department had plans in place to mass-produce the Medium M2 tank. However, the German Blitzkreig through France and the Low Countries convinced the Americans that the lightly-armed and thinly-armoured M2 would be inadequate when the USA inevitably found itself at war with the Germans. Designs for a better-armed and more thickly-armoured medium tank were still at an early stage and so an interim design based on the M2 was seen as a feasible solution. The M3 Medium Tank used many of the components of the M2 but fitted a 75mm dual-purpose gun in the right-hand side sponson with a 37mm in a turret on top of the tank. Both guns had gyro stabilizers to enable the tank to fire on the move, but the limited traverse of the main gun was a limiting factor. However, when the British 8th Army in the Western Desert took delivery in early 1942 of the M3 Medium (known as 'General Grant') they had parity with German armour for the first time in the campaign.

Total production of the M3 Medium reached 6,258, but the majority of the tanks went to America's allies, with the British receiving 2,887 and the Soviet Union 1,386, although 417 of these were lost en-route due to German attacks on the convoys carrying the tanks. The US Army used the M3 Medium (popularly known as the 'General Lee') in North Africa after Operation *Torch* and in limited numbers in the Pacific theatre of operations in 1943. Whilst the British and Commonwealth forces made extensive use of their M3 Grants, the US Army saw them as an interim design and quickly replaced them with the M4 Medium Tank as these became available.

M4 MEDIUM SERIES (GENERAL SHERMAN)

By far the most well-known and ubiquitous tank in the armoury of the US Army of World War II was the M4 Medium Tank, known by the British as the 'Sherman'. Around 50,000 Shermans were produced and distributed, not only for US armed forces (Army and Marines), but large numbers were passed under Lend-Lease to the Americans' allies. The Soviet Union received 2,007 Shermans armed with 75mm guns and 2,095 fitted with the 76mm gun. An additional total of 17,184 went to the western allies of Great Britain and Commonwealth forces such as Canada, Australia and New Zealand and additional tanks went to the Free French and Free Polish.

Initially used in combat by the British 8th Army in North Africa in the summer of 1942 before the second Battle of El Alamein, the Sherman was the first tank in the British army to have a turret-mounted gun capable of firing both armour-piercing and high-explosive rounds. The 8th Army had earlier received the American M3, which also featured a 75mm dual-purpose gun, but as this was mounted in a side sponson with limited traverse it was tactically limited and at best only an interim AFV.

The Sherman was always considered to be reliable and, when it was first introduced, well armed and thickly armoured compared to the majority of enemy Panzers. In the Western Desert the Sherman gave the British parity with German armour for the first time in World War II. The Sherman was superior to the majority of the older German tanks and the equal to the Panzerkampfwagen IV 'Special' that, like the Sherman, mounted a long-barrelled 75mm gun firing medium-velocity shells. The American Army had an inauspicious combat introduction when Shermans of 66 Armoured Regiment, 2 Armored Division, were wiped out by German anti-tank guns near Djebel bou Aoukar. The inexperienced Americans had much to learn and would do so in the long campaigns in Sicily, Italy and northwest Europe, but the Sherman was their work-horse.

The Sherman suffered from two major problems that plagued the vehicle throughout World War II. Whilst the medium-velocity 75mm gun was a match for the Panzers in the desert encounters in late 1942 and early 1943, the appearance of first the German Tigers and then Panthers showed the gun to be inadequate. Even at point-blank range the Sherman's gun could not penetrate the Tiger's thick armour or the front armour of the Panther, whereas both these tanks could pick off a Sherman at 2,000 metres. The Americans worked hard to redress the balance and a programme of replacing the 75mm with a high velocity 76mm was vigorously pursued. When firing high-velocity, armour-piercing M93 rounds the 76mm gun could defeat the Tiger and Panther at over 1,000 metres. However, although this round was rushed into production, it was only available in the last few months of World War II. American anti-tank doctrine was based on using tank destroyers to engage enemy tanks and it was not until the arrival of the M26 Pershing in the closing stages

of the war that the Americans achieved parity with the heavier German armour.

The second issue with the Sherman was the tank's tendency to catch fire when penetrated by an enemy shell. Mostly this was due to the penetrating shell igniting the ammunition stored in the turret or hull. A penetration would often result in flames engulfing the Sherman in a matter of seconds. Being trapped in the confines of a burning tank was the stuff of nightmares for all tank crews. With the Sherman crews it was an occurrence that happened all too often. The Germans referred to British Shermans as 'Tommy Cookers' and with typical gallows humour allied tank crews called them 'Ronsons' after the cigarette lighter that '…lights every time'. To overcome this the American tank manufacturers fitted 'appliqué' armoured plates on the Sherman hull and turret to give the ammunition stowage bins extra protection. Unfortunately this had the opposite effect, as it gave German gunners an aiming point, particularly if a white recognition star had been painted on the plates, as often happened early on in the war. A much better solution was to surround the stowage bins with a water bath. Known as 'wet stowage' this modification reduced the amount of ammunition that could be carried but had a significant impact on the number of fires suffered by Sherman tanks.

The Sherman was produced in a variety of models. Confusingly the second variant, the M4A1, was the first to roll off the production line followed by the M4A2, even though the M4 was designed first. The next variant was the M4A3. The M4A4 Sherman was not used by the US Army but was exported to America's allies. The M4A5 was the nomenclature for the Canadian-built Ram II tank (that resembled the Sherman) and only seventy-five M4A6 tanks were built and none ever saw combat. Within each group there were subdivisions that had an 'E' designation followed by a number (for example, M4A1E1). This 'E' sub-group often denoted an experimental version, but a few such as the M4A3E2 'Jumbo' and the M4A3E8 that used a different suspension were produced in larger numbers than just a few prototypes. There were further varieties within each group of tanks. After experience of combat, major changes were made on the production line. Typical was the change from 'small' to 'large' hatches for the driver and bow-gunner positions. The slope of the front armour was changed and the mantlet significantly altered to reduce shell traps. As explained above, the original 75mm M3 gun was replaced with the 76mm M1 main armament and this could only be installed in a new turret, based on another experimental tank, the T23 Medium Tank.

The rapid expansion of war production after the USA entered World War II caused further variations. Pre-war production of tanks had been limited to the Rock Island arsenal, but to meet the demands of defeating the Axis powers the enormous resources of the US automobile and other engineering facilities were switched to tank production. Ford, Chrysler, Fischer, Baldwin, Lima and Massey-Harris all produced tanks. Although following common designs, different manufacturers might make subtle changes to their versions, so perhaps a lifting hook would be moved an inch or so or a particular ring might be oval rather than round.

Modelling the Sherman is seen by some as a full-time job! There are numerous sites on the internet and on social media devoted to 'Shermania'. The limitations of the size of this book mean that the examples here only scratch the surface. When building the Sherman, look out for the small changes outlined above, as these can prove a minefield for the modelmaker looking to build a Sherman other than straight out of the box.

Medium M4 (Sherman I)

The M4 was the original design but was the final version to enter production, after the M4A1, M4A2 and M4A3, in July 1942. The medium tanks M4 and the M4A1 were mechanically identical and used the same Continental R975-C4 gasoline engine. The major and most obvious difference between the tanks was that the M4 had welded armour plates whereas the M4A1 had a cast upper hull. The engine compartment of the M4 had twin access doors in the rear hull with air cleaners at the top outer corners of the doors, twin square exhaust (muffler) tailpipes at the top of the hull and a steel-covered air intake behind the turret.

Painted in Canadian colours, this Medium M4 has a three-piece transmission cover with grousers (also known as duckbills) fitted to the end of the tracks to improve weight distribution.

The rear of a Sherman showing the square air filters used with the Medium M4.

Type	Production	Numbers	Builders	Features
M4 (75)	July 1942 to January 1944	6,748	PSCC, ALCO, BLW PS, Chrysler	Includes 1,676 M4 Composite
M4 (105)	February to September 1944	800	Chrysler	Revised turret and mantlet
M4 (105) HVSS	September 1944 to March 1945	841	Chrysler	New suspension

Production of the M4

ALCO – American Locomotive
BLW – Baldwin Locomotive Works
PCFC – Pacific Car and Foundry Company
PS – Pullman Standard
PSCC – Pressed Steel Car Company

The early M4s had direct-vision slots in front of the driver and assistant driver but these proved vulnerable and were removed on later models. These direct-vision tanks had what was termed a low-bustle turret, whereas the later versions had a high-bustle turret to clear the periscopes and protectors fitted to the hull hatches of these later tanks. Other changes that occurred as the M4 went through production included the introduction of a single-piece cast transmission housing to replace the three-piece, bolted-together unit. Gun mounts changed from the slim shield of the M34, which was modified to include guards around the barrel, to the wider shield of the M34A1 mount. All M4s were built with dry ammunition stowage and so most had appliqué armour fitted at some time in their existence.

Each tank factory would not unsurprisingly make changes to the original design to ease production. The front glacis plate of the M4 was the most complicated part of the tank to manufacture and so the Chrysler Detroit tank arsenal replaced the welded upper-front hull with a cast glacis. These became known as the Sherman Hybrid or M4 Composite. Around fifty of these tanks were manufactured with the small hatch, but the vast majority had the later large-hatch design. These were the only large-hatch M4s armed with the 75mm gun. The late production M4 models from ALCO were also composite hulls.

The biggest and most obvious change to the M4 came with the introduction of the 105mm howitzer. These tanks retained the high-bustle turrets of the late 75mm-gun tanks, but lacked stabilization and were built without power traverse. The M52 mount had a thicker shield with lifting hooks on each side of howitzer. A second ventilator was added to the rear of the turret roof, and the mount for the .50cal MG was redesigned to fit over this ventilator. The M52 mount was unique, as a dust cover could be fitted – a feature seen on most modern tanks. Early models lacked

the commander's cupola, but these were fitted as they became available. Wet ammunition stowage was never used with 105mm howitzer Shermans – although the ammunition stowage racks were armoured. Appliqué armour was not added, even though the 105mm-armed M4s did not have wet stowage.

The first Sherman – the M4A1

Although the M4 was the original design, it was the M4A1 tank that entered production first in February 1942. The medium tank M4A1 shared many components with the M3 Medium Tank, including the suspension, lower hull, and power train.

The M4A1's cast upper hull gave it distinctive, rounded edges not seen on other M4s and this makes it the easiest Sherman tank to identify. Most M4A1s had single-piece transmission covers and, like the M4, the M4A1 has twin engine access doors in the rear hull and air filters above the top corners of these doors.

A renovated Medium M4 mounting a 105mm Howitzer. This example is in British colours and sits outside a museum in Belgium. Crews often welded spare track links to the front of their tanks to give extra protection.

The early M4A1s had the same suspension as the M3 Medium, with the return roller above the suspension unit rather than the trailing wheel of the M4 bogie.

The M4A1 cast hull is the most obvious difference between this version of the M4 and other versions.

Access to the engine on the M4 and M4A1s was through rear doors that provided only limited access.

Type	Production	Numbers	Builders	Features
M4A1 (75)	February 1942 to December 1943	6,281	PSCC, LLW, PCFC	
M4A1 Grizzly	August to October 1943	188	MLW*	External fittings varied
M4A1 (76) W	January to December 1944	2,171	PSCC	T23 turret. Large front hatches
M4A1 (76) W HVSS	January to July 1945	1,255	PSCC	New suspension

Production of the M4A1

PSCC – Pressed Steel Car Company
LLW – Lima Locomotive Works
PCFC – Pacific Car and Foundry Company
*MLW – Montreal Locomotive Works. The Canadians produced 188 M4A1s known as 'Grizzly 1' (*see* note).

Early M4A1s had twin fixed .30-cal M1919A4 machine guns in the hull, which were operated by the driver, but these were eliminated on tanks built after 6 March 1942. The early M4A1s had spoked idler and road wheels, three-piece differential and final-drive housing, two fuel shutoff valves on the rear deck, removable headlights, vision slots for the drivers in the glacis plate, and the siren was placed on the left-front mudguard. Heavy-duty suspension bogies, with the return roller on the rear of the bogie instead of on top like earlier M3 bogies, were introduced by summer 1942. There was only one turret hatch for the commander with the small oval hatch for the loader entering production in October 1943, with retrofit kits developed for tanks built before the loader's hatch was designed.

The main gun in the first M4A1s was the 75mm M2. This is easily recognized, because to be compatible with the tank's gyrostabilizer it needed double counterweights on the end of the barrel. This was replaced early on with the 75mm M3 gun. Combat experience showed the vulnerability of the M4A1, and 2.5cm (1in) thick appliqué armour plates were welded over the sponson ammunition racks and to the right side of the turret.

In late 1943, M4A1 hulls were changed to incorporate larger drivers' hatches and a thicker 64mm (2.5in) glacis inclined at 47 degrees instead of 56 degrees. The castings themselves on these vehicles were thickened over the vulnerable areas so that the appliqué armour was not required. About 100 M4A1s were built with the 47-degree

Appliqué armour consisted of metal plates welded on to the M4 hull and turrets to give extra protection for the ammunition stowage.

The Slapton Sands M4A1 serves as a memorial to those that died during training exercises for the D-Day landings. Once pulled from the sea, the tank was treated with 'Fertan Rust Converter' to combat the inevitable problem that once the tank was exposed to the air it would quickly rust.

THE SLAPTON SANDS SHERMAN

On the outskirts of the pretty Devon seaside village of Torcross is a large car park that has an unusual war memorial. An M4A1 Duplex Drive Sherman is mounted on a pebble plinth surrounded by a collection of memorials that tell the tank's story and a dedication to the memory of the 946 American Servicemen who lost their lives during Operation *Tiger*, which took place in the English Channel near to where the tank now stands.

The Sherman was recovered from the sea in November 1984, just a little too late for the 40th Anniversary celebrations of the D-Day landings. This was accomplished by the owner of a guesthouse that overlooks the site, the late Ken Small, whose book *The Forgotten Dead* describes his struggles with bureaucracy – and the sea – to literally drag the tank from its watery grave. The book goes into detail about the tragic events that occurred off the Devon coast when a convoy of unescorted landing craft, practising for the forthcoming Operation *Overlord* landings, were attacked by German E-Boats.

There is little remaining to show that this was a DD tank. The only real signs are the remains of the Duplex Drive gear connected to the idler wheels on the rear hull. The propellers and drive shafts are missing, but the sprockets on the rear idlers show that this was a Duplex Drive vehicle. (Although the drive sprocket teeth are still fitted, which, although the norm on British DD tanks, were normally removed from the US version.) This DD Sherman was part of 70th Tank Battalion, which was one of three tank battalions – the others being 741st and 743rd – that were due to be equipped with DD tanks.

Many of the 100 large-hatch M4A1s that were built and armed with a 75mm gun were converted to DD tanks like the one at Slapton Sands. Although the Americans deployed Sherman DD tanks on D-Day, they were launched too far away from the beach and, unlike the tanks in the British sector, they played almost no part in supporting the American troops that were the first to land on Omaha and Utah beaches. The cogs on the rear idlers drove propellers at the rear of the tank.

glacis and dry stowage, and all of these were armed with the 75mm gun M3. Most were converted to swimming 'Duplex Drive' (DD) tanks for use in the Normandy invasion, with one surviving example at Slapton Sands in Devon, where it acts as a memorial for the US Servicemen lost during Operation *Tiger*.

The M4A1(76)W first rolled off the production line in January 1944. The 'W' suffix in the designation indicates 'Wet' stowage, as the main gun ammunition was stored in double-walled boxes with the space between the walls being filled with water. (Ethylene glycol solutions were added to prevent freezing in cold climates, as was Ammudamp rust inhibitor.) The wet stowage was designed to inhibit fires if the ammunition boxes were penetrated by enemy rounds or shrapnel. The 76mm gun was fitted in a new turret that had been developed from the T23 Medium Tank, which never entered production (*see* Chapter 12). The turret of the first M4A1(76) Ws was fitted with a split hatch for the loader, which was replaced with the small oval hatch. The M1A1C 76mm guns had the end of the barrel threaded for a muzzle brake and the M1A2 was fitted with muzzle brakes. The last versions of the M4A1 (76) W had the distinctive HVSS suspension.

This M4 is being renovated, but the size and position of the commander's and the small loader's hatches are self-evident.

THE GRIZZLY SHERMAN

In August 1943 Montreal Locomotive Works in Canada began production of the M4A1. Named the cruiser tank 'Grizzly I' by the Canadians, the first of these was delivered in October. However, only 188 tanks were built, as it became clear that Canadian and British needs would be met by American-manufactured medium tanks. Production was switched to the Sexton self-propelled gun using the same chassis. The Grizzly left the factory with the standard US 13-tooth sprocket, but later Canadian Dry Pin (CDP) tracks and a 17-tooth sprocket were developed, along with heavier-duty bogie units for the Sexton. Later some Grizzlies were converted into the Skink anti-aircraft tank, with a turret mounting four 20mm Polsten guns. Other ways to recognize the Grizzly include a stowage box on the turret bustle, a 2in smoke-bomb thrower in the turret, a floor hatch for the assistant driver, as well as mountings for fire extinguishers and 5-gallon water cans on the hull rear. There was also modified external stowage on the hull's upper hull rear and left side.

The M4A1s built by the Montreal Locomotive Works in Canada were slightly different from those built in the USA. This example at the Muckleburgh Collection in Norfolk has the Canada Dry Pin tracks with 17-tooth drive sprockets. The 'Fury' name seen here precedes the film of that name by many years, as it actually refers to the eponymous dog belonging to the owner's father.

Type	Production	Numbers	Builders	Features
M4A2 (75)	From April 1942 to May 1944	8,053	PUSCC,ALC,BLW, FTA, FMWC	
M4A2 (76) W	From May 1944 to May 1945.	2,915	FTA, PSCC	T23 Turret. Large front hatches
M4A2 (76) W HVSS				New suspension

The Medium M4A2, the first welded-hull Sherman to enter service

The M4A2 was Sherman III in the British nomenclature style and used the General Motors 6046 engine (two GM 6-71 General Motors Diesel units). The M4A2 was not used by the US Army, but found favour with the US Marine Corps and was widely exported to the armies of USSR, Britain, France and Poland. The Marine Corps only ever used the 75mm gun-armed M4A2s.

Production of the M4A2

PUSCC – Pullman Standard Car Company
ALC – American Locomotive Company
BLW – Baldwin Locomotive Works
FTA – Fisher Tank Arsenal
FMWC – Federal Machine and Welder Company
PSCC – Pressed Steel Car Company

The Medium M4A2 closely resembled the M4, with the main external difference being the grilles over the engine on the rear deck of the M4A2. These engine access grille doors were approximately as wide as the turret bustle and were the only means of accessing the engine, as there were no rear access doors to the engine compartment. There are many other small variations but these are dependent on the manufacturer. However, the rear hull plate extends further than on the M4 on all models. All of the US Marine Corps tanks were small hatch with the glacis plate sloped at 57 degrees.

Tanks used by the US Marine Corps that operated in the Pacific theatre of operations look very different from the US Army tanks that were used in Europe. Lacking effective tanks and anti-tank guns in any of the campaigns, the Japanese had to resort to attacking American armour with massed infantry attacks armed with explosive-shaped charges. The US Army and Marines attached spaced armour in the form of wooden planks or corrugated iron to defeat the shaped charges and covered hatches with mesh and nails to stop the enemy gaining access or placing charges on more vulnerable parts.

Medium M4A3 (Sherman IV)

The M4A3 was fitted with a 500hp Ford GAA V8 petrol engine that had been designed specifically for this AFV. Most of the M4A3s built were used by the US Army and Marines.

Production of the M4A3

Medium M4A3 (75) turrets did not have the loader's hatch. The early M4A3 (75) Ws all featured the oval loader's hatch, but were fitted with the split hatch for the commander due to shortages of the turret cupola. Early M4A3 (76) W had the circular split loader's hatch, but this was replaced by the oval hatch in later models.

The first M4A3 (105) lacked a commander's vision cupola, but later versions had this fitted. Powered traverse was not incorporated until after World War II in Europe was over and an armoured cover for the direct sight telescope in the mantlet was developed in late production vehicles to protect the turret interior from small arms fire.

Following experience against heavily armoured German tanks, it was clear that the US Army needed a heavy tank. Once it became clear that

Type	Production	No	Builders	Features
M4A3 (75)	June 1942 to September 1943	1,690	Ford	
M4A3 (75) W	February 1944 to March 1945	3,071	Fisher (Grand Blanc)	Wet stowage, loader's hatch and 47-degree glacis
M4A3E2 (Jumbo)	May 1944 to July 1944	254	Fisher (Grand Blanc)	Armour increased to 100mm hull and 150mm turret
M4A3 (76) W	March 1944 to December 1944	1,925	Fisher, (Grand Blanc) Chrysler (Detroit Arsenal)	Wet stowage, large hatches and 47-degree glacis
M4A3 (76) HVSS	August 1944 to April 1945	2,617	Chrysler (Detroit Arsenal)	New suspension and T80 tracks
M4A3 (105)	May 1944 to September 1944	500	Chrysler (Detroit Arsenal)	Close support 105mm Howitzer and revised turret
M4A3 (105) HVSS	September 1944 to June 1945	2,539	Chrysler (Detroit Arsenal)	New suspension and T80 tracks

the T26 would not be available until 1945, a compromise design in the form of a heavily armoured M4A3 was proposed. The M4A3E2 entered production in May 1944 and was delivered just after D-Day. Additional hull armour increased the thickness to 100mm and 150mm on the turret. At best it was a compromise design and only 254 were built. The 'Jumbo' was fitted with a 75mm gun, but some versions had a 76mm gun fitted in the field.

The final 76mm version of the M4A3 used the Horizontal Volute Suspension System, which increased the Sherman's weight by 2,950lb with T66 single-pin track and 4,780lb with T84 double-pin track. The new HVSS allowed the installation of wider tracks, so although overall weight increased with the new suspension the tank's ground pressure significantly decreased and coupled with new shock absorbers mounted on the bogies the M4A3 HVSS was a smoother ride. The prototype tank had the suffix E8 and a popular theory is that the tanks were referred to as 'Easy Eight'. The M4A3 HVSS 76 W marked the pinnacle of Sherman production, with this version of the Sherman remaining in front-line service well after World War II.

BUILDING THE M3 MEDIUM TANK

M3A1 in 1/72 scale

Mirage M3A1 Medium Tank No 72803
RB 75mm M2 L/31 and 37mm US Tank Gun Barrel set for M3 Lee 72B60

For many years the only version of the M3 Medium Tank available in small scale was from Airfix. The Poland-based Mirage company produces a number of US Army tanks, including the M3 and M3A1 Medium Tanks. The latter is the most unusual, as like the M4A1 Medium the hull was cast and has a unique round shape. The Mirage kit was built straight out of the box with the only changes being to replace the two guns with RB metal barrels. The kit includes a small etched-brass fret. Unfortunately with the doors closed most of the etched brass is not seen, but the brush guards provided are easy to fold and look neat. The kit was finished in olive drab and decals provided were used to represent an early production model used at the Armored Force School at Fort Knox in 1942.

The Airfix M3 General Lee in 1/76 scale. This depicts a tank in use by the British. Whilst most of the M3 Mediums in use by the British were Grants, they also had a few M3 Lee tanks.

The M3A1 Medium Tank from Mirage depicts the cast-hull version of the tank. The model depicts a tank used by the Armored Forces Training School.

The unusual layout of the M3 Medium is shown to good effect here. The sponson-mounted 75mm gun was at best an interim measure and put the tank at a tactical disadvantage compared to the M4 Medium with its turret-mounted 75mm gun.

BUILDING THE M4 MEDIUM TANK

There are many models of the M4 available in all the popular scales.

M4 – 75mm in 1/48 scale

Tamiya 1/48 M4 Sherman Item 32505

RB M4 Sherman 75mm M3 gun barrel 48B05

RB 7.62 mm Browning M1919 48B34

ABER etched parts for M4 Sherman (Early
     Production) 48003

Dartmoor Military Models DMM-48M-014

The Tank Craft series of books is a great reference source for military modelmakers. The series is dominated by German armour, but there are a few books about allied armour and I used an example in the colour sheets as the basis for an M4 75mm of 66th Armored Regiment, 2nd Armored Division in France, Summer 1944. The Tamiya kits are very modeller-friendly and easy to build. The 1/48 tank kits mostly have metal chassis and these add weight to the model that makes it sit better. The drive sprockets are fitted to the chassis through a soft plastic bushing, so that when fitting the track links the sprocket can be turned to ensure everything lines up.

The Tamiya kits are really well engineered. The drive sprockets fit the chassis through a soft plastic bushing. This enables the modelmaker to fit the sprocket to the chassis and then turn the sprocket to facilitate fitting the tracks.

The periscopes shown here in the driver's hatch were relatively delicate and metal guards were fitted to protect them.

The rear lights were also protected, as can be seen on this museum example. The rear light guards provided with the kit are often quite thick and many modelmakers replace them with some etched brass examples in order to look really authentic.

The delicate periscope guards and brush guards for the headlamps on the model are from the Aber etched brass set.

A completed model M4 based on a colour illustration in Dennis Oliver's superb Sherman Tank US Army North Western Europe, 1944–1945.

The kit was built very much out of the box. The etched brass set from Aber is very comprehensive and includes periscope covers, headlight brush guards and protectors for the rear lights. The M4 was painted and weathered as shown in Chapter 4.

There is no readily available Calliope T34 rocket launcher in 1/48 scale, so I decided to build one from scratch. The model would be the early version based on the M4 and the base vehicle was a combination of parts left over from other projects (although a Tamiya or Hobby Boss kit could provide a suitable base). The Hobby Boss suspension was

fitted to a Tamiya chassis and a Hobby Boss one-piece transmission case suitably modified to fit. The turret had some appropriate etched brass added and the loader's periscope removed, as well as an etched brass detail added, as the firing wires were fed through this hole on the real vehicle.

Plans from George Bradford's *Allied Armoured Fighting Vehicles – Plans in 1/72 Scale* were enlarged to 1/48 scale and plastic card cut to produce the support structure for the rocket tubes. Details were added using parts of an etched-brass fret and thin wire wound around some brass rod made the distinctive spring assembly.

THE AIRFIX SHERMAN

Many modelmakers from the 1960s and 1970s will recall with some affection the Airfix Sherman tank. This first appeared in 1961 and, alongside the Panther and Churchill, was one of the first tanks produced by Airfix and consequently one of the first mass-produced plastic model tanks in the world. The early Airfix cardboard headers for the plastic bags were simple drawings, but later versions of the Airfix artwork are seen as some the finest paintings of military aircraft and vehicles ever to grace the box art of a construction kit. However, the early Sherman tank artwork caused some controversy, as unmistakable in the foreground is the body of a dead soldier. As the packaging changed, so less and less of the corpse was seen, until he eventually disappeared altogether.

The packaging of the Airfix Sherman with the dead German in the bottom left of the picture. Note the scale has now leapt to 1/72 scale, although the kit has not changed. This kit was produced for the US market.

M4 Calliope in 1/48 scale

Upper hull: Tamiya 1/48 M4 Sherman Item 32505

Lower hull: Hobby Boss US M4 Tank 84802

RB M4 Sherman 75mm M3 gun barrel 48B05

RB 7.62mm Browning M1919 48B34

Hauler etched parts for M4 Sherman HLX48001

Rocket tubes – Plastruct – Round tubing TBFS 3

The rocket launch tubes were made from Plastruct tubing cut to length and then glued together as pairs before mounting on the structure. The launch tubes' locking mechanisms were added from plastic rod and trimmed sprue. Etched-brass details were added to complete the construction phase. This unusual Sherman was completed in olive drab following the techniques outlined in Chapter 4. Each rocket tube was fired electrically, and to finish the model off thin wire was added to each tube and then the resulting loom fed through the hole where

A scratch-built frame for the Sherman Calliope. It mainly consists of plastic card with wire wound around a brass rod and offcuts from an etched brass fret to make the detailed parts. The rod is a temporary measure to check the fit.

CALLIOPE SHERMAN

Following reports from front-line troops, the United States Ordnance Department recognized the need to provide assault troops with more firepower through the use of unguided rockets. The T34 Calliope Rocket Launcher carried sixty 4.5in tubes that were mounted initially on the M4 Medium. The name 'Calliope' is derived from a musical instrument, also known as the steam organ, which had similar parallel pipes. The system was mounted on the turret and elevation set through an arm linking the T34 and the main gun. The T34 was available for the Normandy campaign, but concerns over transporting the top-heavy tank meant that it was not used for the invasion. The early version had to jettison the T34 before the tank's main armament could be fired and so the modified version fitted to the Medium M4A3 had the T34 connected to the mantlet rather than the barrel and could fire the main gun with the tubes attached, but at limited elevation. Plans to use the Sherman Calliope in December 1944 were curtailed due to the German counter-offensive in the Ardennes, but in February 1945 small numbers of T34 tubes were fitted to 3rd Army tanks and were used during the push into Germany. Each rocket contained the same amount of explosives as a 105mm howitzer shell and sixty rockets landing in an area would have been devastating. However, the system was crude and inaccurate and so probably of limited effectiveness, although it probably had a greater psychological impact than as an area fire weapon.

the loader's periscope would normally be fitted. (Later versions fed the cables through the hole for the antenna mount.) The model was only lightly weathered.

At the time of writing there is no injection-moulded kit of the M4 Hybrid tank in 1/48 scale. Friendship Models produces a suitable hull in resin designed to fit on the Tamiya M4 kit. The lower chassis is from Tamiya and made from metal and the weight makes the tank sit well on the tracks. The single-piece transmission cover from Hobby Boss was cemented in place. The wheels in the Tamiya kit are the early spoked type and I replaced them with the spares from a Hobby Boss kit.

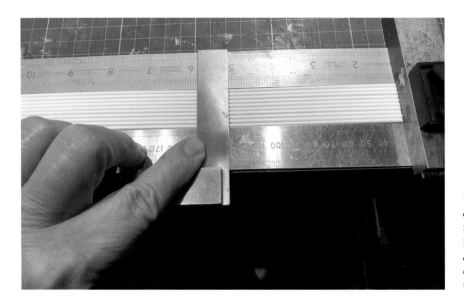

Two metal rulers and a block were clamped to a cutting board. The tubes all need to be an identical length, as even a millimetre out will be obvious.

The model was coated with a thin layer of satin varnish before being lightly weathered.

The rocket tubes were glued together in pairs. Tamiya Extra Thin Cement ran neatly between the tubes and set quickly. The pairs of tubes were now cemented to the frame. Thirty-six Tubes were above the frame and two groups of twelve tubes below the frame.

The tank was painted in US olive drab and weathered as outlined in Chapter 4. No markings were added.

M4 Composite in 1/48 scale

Upper hull: Friendship Models Hybrid Sherman

Lower hull and suspension: Tamiya 1/48 M4 Sherman Item 32505

Wheels: Hobby Boss US M4A3 (76) W Tank 84805

Tracks: OKB Grigorov 1/48 Tracks for M4 family T54E1

Turret: Friendship Models M4 Turret

RB M4 Sherman 75mm M3 gun barrel 48B05

RB 7.62mm Browning M1919 48B34

Hauler etched parts for M4 Sherman HLX48001

Hauler lights and periscope guards for US vehicles HLX48265

I built the suspension units and then used an epoxy resin to secure these suspension units in place. Once complete these were left overnight to dry. The tracks from OKB Grigorov were fitted after the drive sprockets in the Tamiya kit were made around 1mm wider, so that the sprockets were wide enough to accept the tracks.

The M4 Hybrid. The Friendship Model's resin upper hull mates neatly with the Tamiya M4 chassis. The suspension units are from Tamiya, with spare wheels from a Hobby Boss kit.

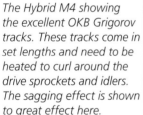

The Hybrid M4 showing the excellent OKB Grigorov tracks. These tracks come in set lengths and need to be heated to curl around the drive sprockets and idlers. The sagging effect is shown to great effect here.

The lower hull, suspension and tracks were set aside to dry and then the upper hull was glued in place using epoxy resin. The fit of the Friendship Models hull is really good and the only change I made was to replace the resin mudguards with some from etched brass and used the large hatches from the Hobby Boss kit. The turret is also from Friendship Models and is resin. I added hatches, hatch ring and the rear part of the mantlet from a Tamiya kit. Periscope and periscope covers as well as sighting vanes on the turret and brush guards for the headlights were added from the Hauler etched-brass detailing sets. The front mantlet is from a Hobby Boss kit, installed once the RB 75mm gun was fitted as was the hull machine gun, also from RB.

The completed M4 Hybrid painted following the techniques outlined in Chapter 4. The crew figure is from the excellent Dartmoor Models range.

M4 Crocodile in 1/76 scale

M4 Tank Airfix kit A01303V

Flame trailer from Airfix Churchill Crocodile
    A02321V

The Airfix M4 Sherman first appeared in 1961 and by modern standards it is very inaccurate, with an under-sized turret. The tank was built as set out in the instructions with a replacement turret from a Nitto kit and the awful soft plastic tracks replaced with tracks from a Revell Firefly kit. The moulded-on tools were scraped off and detailed parts from other kits used to replace the headlamps. Appliqué armour was added to the hull sides from plastic card. The commander's cupola and a 0.5in-cal machine gun came from the spares box.

The flame trailer in the Airfix Churchill Crocodile is quite accurate, with a few detail changes. A hatch was added to the back half of the trailer and metal handles added from wire. The towing arm on top of the trailer had the locating tab removed and the arm moved back. A small rod passing through the towing eye was fixed to the

body of the trailer. Two stabilizing legs were built from scrap plastic and metal rod and held in place on the back of the trailer. The trailer was fixed just off-centre to the rear of the Sherman hull. Plastic trunking was added to the side of the Sherman to represent the armoured box that protected the fuel lines and the flame gun built by adding some details to the gun in the Churchill kit.

A flame-thrower trailer from a British Churchill Crocodile was photographed in the yard at the RAC Tank Museum at Bovington. This type of trailer was used by the US Army in very small numbers to produce the Sherman Crocodile.

The US Army had a few Sherman Crocodile flame-thrower tanks that saw limited action at the end of the campaign in Europe. This model uses the Airfix Churchill Crocodile trailer and a heavily modified Airfix Sherman.

M4 Composite in 1/72 scale

Rear hull: Trumpeter M4 Mid Production Kit 07223

Front hull and suspension: Italeri M4A1 Sherman Kit 7003

Tracks: OKB Grigorov tracks for M4 Family

Trunking: Heller M4 Sherman 'D-Day' Ref 79892

The Trumpeter M4 kit in 1/72 scale has a very inaccurate hull with the glacis sloping at an angle that is far too shallow. However, it does make a good basis for the M4 composite or hybrid tank. The suspension lower hull and front glacis from the excellent Italeri kit were mated with the Trumpeter hull. The join between the two kits needed quite a lot of filler, which was added and then filed smooth to give a seamless joint. The Trumpeter turret was added with open hatches and lifting eyes installed using suitably shaped brass wire. The cast hull front was given a thin coat of Mr Surfacer 1200 to emphasize the cast finish. The model would represent a US Marine

Corps tank and wading trunking from the Heller M4 kit was added. Appliqué armour from plastic card was added and, after the model had been primed in black, a base coat of olive drab was sprayed over the model. Once the coats were dry, streaking to the turret and hull sides was applied and this was toned down with a green filter. The completed model was mounted on a small base with US Marine crew figures and 0.50cal machine gun added.

The Trumpeter rear upper hull was mated with an Italeri lower hull and cast glacis plate to produce an M4 Hybrid. Italeri suspension was fitted and the turret from the Trumpeter kit had open hatches added from the Italeri kit. The front mud guards were from an etched brass set and some filler was needed to mate the guards to the upper hull.

Wading trunking from the Heller M4 kit was added before the model was given a black-primer coat and a base coat of olive drab. The completed model represents one of the Hybrid M4 Medium Tanks used by the US Marine Corps.

BUILDING THE M4 A1 MEDIUM TANK

The market is well served with the distinctive cast-hull M4A1 in all scales. Both the 75mm and 76mm versions are available in 1/72 and 1/48, as well as in 1/35 scale.

M4A1 75mm in 1/48 scale

Tamiya 1/48 M4A1 Sherman Item 32523

RB M4 Sherman 75mm M3 gun barrel 48B05

RB 7.62mm Browning M1919 48B34

Hauler etched parts for M4A1 HLX 48075

Dartmoor Military Models DMM048M.014

I decided to build an early version of the M4A1 of A Company 741st Tank Battalion that was photographed in Germany in the Spring of 1945. Unusually the tank still carries the Culin hedgerow cutter (sometimes called the Rhino tank) from the Normandy battles and has wire mesh along the hull and turret held in place with cable hawser that has been welded in place. The tank is depicted in Tank Craft 11 *Sherman Tanks – US Army North-Western Europe 1944–1945*, one of the few books in the wonderful Tank Craft series that is devoted to Allied armour. The Tamiya kit is the basis for the model and is built virtually out of the box. The only major surgery carried out was to replace the front mudguards (fenders) with etched brass. The wire mesh used on the real thing to hold in place vegetation for camouflage was from a plastic mesh bag that held garlic (after it was washed!) and the cable from single-core wire. I decided to scratch-build the Culin device, but I found out later that Hauler make a photo-etched Culin that is available as an after-market accessory in 1/48 scale. This was glued directly to the front of the tank – just as the real thing was welded to the front of the M4A1.

The tank was painted in olive drab with tools, jerry cans and other stowage added from the kit and the spares box. The commander figure is from the excellent Dartmoor range, suitably painted and holding a map from the Quarter Master range. I wanted to depict a really muddy tank as it may have appeared after putting the Culin device into use and so after painting and minimal weathering I dipped a large stiff paint brush in some 'mud mixture' (enamel paint and weathering powders) and holding the brush a few centimetres from the tank pulled back the bristles and let fly. The 'mud' produced a satisfying splatter pattern on the front of the tank. The finished model was secured to the base using magnets.

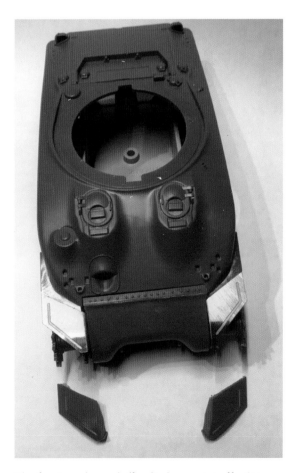

The front mud guards (fenders) were cut off using a razor saw, as the plastic in the Tamiya kit is thick compared to the real thing. They were replaced with items from the Haulier set, which are thin, like the real thing.

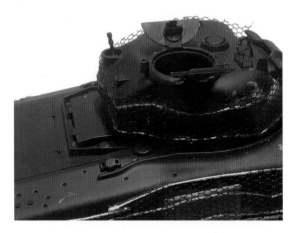

The M4A1 model is based on a tank that had mesh fixed to the hull sides and turret. This mesh was held in place by welding a metal cable to the tank and attaching the mesh by using twisted wire.

The front of the tank was weathered to represent a vehicle that had just cut through a bocage hedgerow. To replicate the mud on the front of the tank a stiff brush was loaded with a suitable mud mixture and then with the brush close to the tank the bristles were pulled back to let fly with the mud.

The completed 1/48 scale M4A1 Tamiya kit with extra detailing and scratch-built Culin prongs with an unusual mesh fixed to the hull sides and turret. The front of the tank was plastered with mud to simulate a tank that had just ploughed through a hedgerow.

The Culin Hedgerow Cutter was a modification that used German beach obstacles to provide a means of cutting through the high banks of hedges in Normandy, which the French call bocage. Hauler produce an etched-brass Culin Hedgerow Cutter kit in 1/48 scale designed for the Tamiya Sherman.

The M4A1 in action with accompanying infantry. The mesh used to hold foliage in place is shown to great effect here.

PHOTO ETCH

Photo Etch is now readily available for military vehicle detailing. Although small-scale accessories for 1/76 and 1/72 are nowhere near as abundant as in 1/35 scale, Photo Etch in 1/48 scale is becoming more popular. For depicting thin plates and items such as brush guards and periscope covers the fine detail that etched brass offers beats injection-moulded plastic and resin hands down. However, for items like tool handles, folding etched-brass shapes to make a bulky item just does not work for me. Sometimes even etched brass does not provide what you need but everyday items perhaps can. Tin foil containers from takeaway meals are an excellent source of thin and flexible metal sheets and the clear plastic used for some hobby products is a good source of windscreens. For the model here I used the mesh bag that held a garlic bulb as the source of scale mesh. There are lots of materials out there that can be useful; it is just a case of seeing the potential in mundane, everyday items.

The Tamiya range of 1/48 vehicles is the most extensive in this scale, but other mainstream manufacturers have also produced a few models in the same scale. Hobby Boss makes a few Sherman models that fill some of the gaps left by Tamiya. The Hobby Boss kits are much cheaper than the Tamiya kits, but lack the die-cast metal chassis and the link and length tracks of the Tamiya kits. Generally the Hobby Boss kits are not as accurate as the Tamiya models and so need some work to bring them up to a reasonable standard. We will explore the M4A3 kit later on, but the M4A1 (76) W kit is generally acceptable, apart from the turret, which is the wrong shape. This can be corrected by cutting and filling the Hobby Boss turret, but for this build I was fortunate enough to get

---

M4A1 (76) W in 1/48 scale – 1

Hobby Boss 1/48 M4A1 Sherman 84801

Bandai 1/48 M4A3 76mm Kit 058264 (turret) (discontinued)

Aber US 76mm M1A2 barrel 48 L-26

RB 7.62mm Browning M1919 48B34

Hauler etched parts for M4A1 HLX 48075

Hauler Browning M2 .50 calibre machine gun HLX 48195

OKB Grigorov 1/48 tracks for M4 family T54E1

Dartmoor Military Models DMM048M.014

Tamiya US Army Infantry GI Set Item 32513

---

hold of an old Bandai 1/48 kit of the M4A3 (76) W and the T23 turret in this kit is much more accurate for the 76mm-armed Shermans.

The Hobby Boss kit was built as set out in the kit instructions with the soft plastic tracks being replaced by the superb tracks from OKB Grigorov. Etched-brass detailing such as brush guards, periscope covers, rear light protectors and periscopes were added. The Bandai turret was coated with Mr Surfacer to give a cast effect and the 76mm main gun and M1917 0.3in cal machine gun added. The 0.5in-cal HMG is made out of resin and photo-etched brass and is a mini-project in itself. The model was painted in an olive drab and black camouflage scheme used for Operation

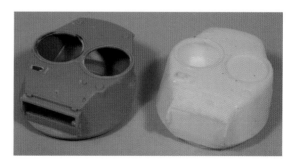

The Hobby Boss T23 turret is the wrong shape, being too wide at the front and too narrow at the rear. I used the Bandai turret as the master to cast my own more-accurate turrets.

The M4A1 (76) W in 1/48 showing the OKB Grigorov tracks and photo-etched details. The turret is from a Bandai kit with some Mr Surfacer 1200 applied to give the turret a cast effect.

The completed M4A1 (76) W from Hobby Boss. The tank crew figures are from the excellent Dartmoor Military Models range. The infantry figures are based on the Tamiya US Army Infantry GI Set with new heads, helmets and weapons from a variety of sources.

The 0.5in calibre Heavy Machine Gun was fitted to many US tanks – primarily as an air defence weapon, although it was frequently used against enemy ground targets. This example is from Haulier and features etched-brass detailing and resin parts.

M4A1 (76) W in 1/48 scale – 2

Bandai 1/48 M4A1 76mm Kit 058281 (discontinued)

Aber US 76mm M1A2 barrel 48 L-26

RB 7.62mm Browning M1919 48B34

Hauler etched parts for M4A1 HLX 48075

OKB Grigorov 1/48 Tracks for M4 family T54E1

Tamiya US Army Infantry GI Set Item 32513

Cobra. I added crew from Dartmoor Models with US infantry from Tamiya in a variety of poses. The finished model was then added to a base with supporting infantry.

The 1/48 scale Bandai 'Pin Point' armour kits were first available in the early 1970s around the same time that Tamiya were introducing their 1/35-scale models. They were revolutionary for their day, featuring a level of detail that was new to a modelmaking public used to Airfix military models, including interior detail and an engine. Today these kits are hard to find and exchange hands on various online auction sites for large sums. Many go to kit collectors rather than model builders. Compared to modern kits, the small parts of the Bandai kits lack fine detail and often have a lot of flash with the plastic being quite brittle. However, the overall dimensions measure up well with the models catching the look of the real thing and the kits do cover versions of the Sherman not available elsewhere in 1/48 scale.

I built the kit out of the box but discarded many of the smaller parts. The hull was completed with

The Bandai large-hatch Shermans first appeared on the shelves of hobby shops nearly fifty years ago. Although they are accurate in terms of dimensions and shape, the plastic is thick compared to more modern kits and fine detail is not there. For this build I replaced the Bandai suspension with some modified spares from a Hobby Boss kit.

etched brass headlamp brush guards and periscope protectors. The Bandai kit suspension is not very detailed and for all its faults the Hobby Boss suspension is more accurate and detailed. (The Hobby Boss kits come with many spare parts to make different suspension types.) Tracks from OKB Grigorov were added and the grousers were left in place. The model was painted as set out in Chapter 4 and a crew figure from a Tamiya kit added to complete the model.

A rear view of the Bandai M4A1 (76mm) W kit in 1/48 scale with suspension units from Hobby Boss to replace the Bandai units, as the latter are not very detailed.

The completed modified Bandai M4A1 (76mm) W. Painting details can be found in Chapter 4. Tracks from OKB Grigorov were used to replace the 'rubber band' tracks that come with the kit. The crew figure is from Tamiya.

M4A1 (75) in 1/72 scale – 1

Chassis and suspension: Mirage M3 General Lee No. 72801

Hull: Friendship Models M4A1 Direct Vision

Turret: Trumpeter No. 07223 M4 Sherman Mid-Production

Main gun: RB 75 mm Gun RB

Hauler etched parts for M4A1 HLX 48075

Tracks: OKB Grigorov 1/72 Tracks for M4 family

Periscope: Wee Friends WBM72014 WWII US M6 Periscopes for Sherman

The earliest versions of the Sherman used the suspension units that had been designed for the M3 Medium Tanks, with the return roller over the centre of the bogie assembly. All later versions used the M4 suspension units that had the trailing bogie. The M4A1 depicted would be a very early version that used the M3 suspension units with a cast hull that included direct-vision slots for the driver and co-driver. The direct-vision tanks were phased out early in production over fears that the slots would render the tank vulnerable at the hull front and the crew had to rely on periscopes or an open hatch with the driver's head exposed. The lower chassis and suspension units came from the Mirage General Lee kit. This is a really nice kit and I hesitated to use just half the kit, but there are few 1/72-scale M3 Medium Tank kits available and the Mirage kit is probably the best. Tracks were added from the OKB Grigorov set. The upper hull is a cast-resin item from Friendship Models and, as with all other kits from Friendship Models, the fit of resin to the plastic kit is almost perfect. The turret is from the Trumpeter kit, with a scratch-built mantlet added. Lifting eyes and brush guards came from the detailing set and the periscope in the commander's hatch is another from Friendship

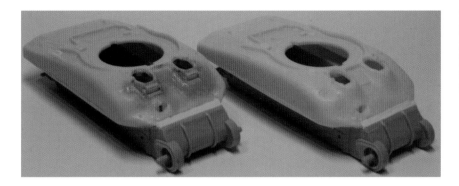

Two M4A1 hulls from Friendship Models. The direct-vision version is on the left with a mid-production hull on the right.

The Mirage M3 bogies with the OKB Grigorov tracks are a good combination. The tank was painted olive drab and then a camouflage scheme of yellow ochre added. This scheme was widely used in Sicily. The streaking effect is obvious here and the addition of weathering pigments toned down this effect, giving the model a dusty appearance.

M4A1 (76) W in 1/72 scale

Lower hull, suspension and tracks: UM Sherman with Mine Exploder T1E3 No 221

Upper hull: Italeri M4A1 Sherman Kit 7003

Turret: Dragon M4A3 (76) W VVSS Sherman Armor Pro 7576

Hauler etched parts for M4A1 HLX 48075

Models. The Sherman was painted in olive drab and ochre in a scheme used during the invasion of Sicily, as set out in Chapter 4. After adding stowage the tank was given a dusting of pigment powders to represent a tank used in the dry conditions of Operation *Husky*. I am not a great fan of dusting pigments, but to represent a tank in desert or arid conditions they do produce a good weathering effect.

The rounded hull of the M4A1 with the 76mm-armed T23 turret make an interesting version of the Sherman that in 1/72 scale is available from Dragon and Trumpeter. I had a spare turret from the Dragon M4A3 kit and decided to combine it with the Italeri M4A1 kit as an exercise in combining components from different kits. Most of the lower suspension is donated by the UM kit, with the bogie units from another donor kit that were less complicated to assemble than the UM version. The Italeri upper hull has the large hatches of the later M4A1 that was used with the 76mm turret. It would have been possible to use all of the Italeri chassis, but the UM kit comes with link and length tracks rather than the Italeri 'rubber bands'. The

The M4A1 (76) W is the result of combining three different kits with parts from the spares box. Nothing goes to waste, as the remaining parts were reconfigured into different models.

The M4A1 (76) W is given a coat of black primer followed by olive drab with black stripes used on US AFVs before Operation Cobra. The completed model in 1/72 is a unique version of the Sherman that is not available as a single kit.

turret from the Dragon kit was available, as the hull had been used with a 75mm turret of a US Marine Corps M4A3. The Culin Hedgerow Cutter had been in the spares box for some years and is from a manufacturer that has long ceased trading. After priming with black AK Interactive Primer, the tank was given a coat of olive drab. This tank was then given a black stripe camouflage pattern and weathered as shown in Chapter 4.

BUILDING THE M4 A2 MEDIUM TANK

Some 75mm M4A2 Mediums are available in 1/72 and 1/35 scale, but there is nothing from the main manufacturers in 1/48 scale. So, if you want to build an M4A2 in 1/48 scale, you either have to scratch-build the upper hull or do as I did and use the hull from Friendship Models.

M4A2 75mm in 1/48 scale

Chassis: Hobby Boss M4A1 (76mm)
  W Sherman 84801

Upper Hull: Friendship Models 1/48 scale
  M4A2 upper hull

Turret: Tamiya M4A1 Item 32523

Tracks: OKB Grigorov 1/48 Tracks for M4
  family T54E1

RB M4 Sherman 75mm M3 gun barrel 48B05

RB 7.62mm Browning M1919 48B34

Hauler etched parts for M4A1 HLX 48075

Additional armour – thin wood veneer

Scratch-built wading trunking and external
  water tank

The M4A2 was built combining a number of different kits with the Hobby Boss M4A1 providing the chassis and suspension units. This was assembled following the kit instructions. The Friendship Models upper hull is made in resin and is a really good fit for the Hobby Boss chassis. The small hatches from the Tamiya M4A1 were added to the hull with some plastic strip used to provide the hinges. The turret came from the Tamiya M4A1 kit, as it has no loader's hatch. The turned-metal gun barrel and coaxial machine gun were inserted through the mantlet, which was then secured to the front of the turret. The commander's split-hatch covers were cemented in the open position and etched brass details added from the Hauler set. The additional plank armour was made from some thin wood veneer from an art shop. A blunt scriber was used to produce the plank effect and bolt heads from plastic rod added. Rear wading trunking was made from plastic card based on a drawing from the internet. This was capped with some mesh from Eduard. Plastic strip cut to appropriate lengths was used to provide the supporting brackets. An external water tank was scratch-built from some plastic tube with details added from scrap plastic. The OKB Grigorov tracks were added before painting.

The only US troops to use the Medium M4A2 were the Marine Corps. The wooden planks seen here are made of thin wooden veneer, available from good art shops. The tank combines the Hobby Boss M4A1 kit and a resin after-market kit from Friendship Models for the upper hull. The fit is good and the detail on the resin kit as good as you will find on many plastic injection-moulded kits.

Probably the best book available about armour in the Pacific theatre is *The Sherman in the Pacific War 1943–45* by Raymond Giuliani. It is very difficult to find and not cheap, but is a superb collection of photographs of Shermans with some excellent colour illustrations. There are several pictures of an M4A2 (75) of the 4th Marine Tank Battalion that served in Saipan in 1944 and these were the inspiration for this model. After applying a black primer coat, the basecoat of Tamiya XF 61 Dark Green was sprayed over the tank. The splinter pattern on the turret and wading trunk was applied using a fine brush with fine lines running out of the blobs to depict the painting of the real tank with a coarse brush. Painted tools were added to the rear deck from the Tamiya kit and the 0.5in calibre HMG added to the turret with the commander figure temporarily inserted to make sure the HMG was in the right place. The real crew were clearly keen that everyone knew their pet name for the tank, as the words 'King Kong' are painted six times on the tank. These

were clearly applied freehand on the real M4A2, so a fine brush and some white enamel paint were used to apply the name. The tank was weathered as set out at Chapter 4.

I had decided that 'King Kong' would be depicted in a Pacific island diorama with the tank parked up next to an abandoned Japanese artillery position with two groups of US Marines: one group sheltering next to the tank and the second

It was not unusual for Marine Corps tanks to carry names. Often all the tanks in a unit would use the same first letter in the name. 'King Kong' was applied by hand on the real thing and on the model.

A completed Medium M4A2 showing the wooden planking and sheets used to give protection against hollow-charge weapons used by the Japanese.

Once completed the M4A2 was given a coat of black primer and then painted in olive green. The turret has a series of ochre blotches that look as if they were applied by a thick brush on the real AFV. US Marine Corps tanks often carried cylindrical tanks of fresh water that could be used by the crew and accompanying marines, as shown here.

A completed model of 'King Kong' with accompanying US Marines representing a tank used during the battles on Saipan in 1944.

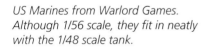

US Marines from Warlord Games. Although 1/56 scale, they fit in neatly with the 1/48 scale tank.

US Marines advancing past an overrun Japanese artillery position. The gun is a 3D-printed 105mm from Shapeways; whilst it does not bear close scrutiny, it looks reasonable in the background.

group with laden packs moving through the artillery dugout and taking up positions near the Sherman. The figures are 28mm US Marines from Warlord. Although they are 1/56 scale, they fit in well with the 1/48-scale tank.

The Heller Shermans are among the best available in 1/72 scale. Although quite hard to find, they are very reasonably priced and come with lots of extra parts to make a variety of versions. The Heller M4A2 is the only version of this tank available in 1/72 in injection-moulded plastic. The kit was built virtually out of the box, the only

---

M4A2 75mm in 1/72 scale

Tank: Heller M4A2 Sherman 'Division Leclerc' Ref 79894

Tracks: OKB Grigorov 1/72 tracks for M4 family

RB M4 Sherman 75mm M3 gun barrel

Hauler etched parts for M4A1 HLX 48075

Additional armour – thin wood veneer

Scratch-built wading trunking

---

additions being some etched-brass guards over the rear lights, an etched-brass sighting vane and some new lifting brackets from an UM kit. The turret hatches were replaced with an all-round vision cupola from a Friendship Models kit with a plastic hatch from a Hasegawa kit. The US Marines added protection to the suspension from long wooden poles that were replicated on the model using plastic rod. Track plates from OKB Grigorov were added to the sides of the hull and the turret and the build was finished with some scratch-built rear trunking. The black primer coat was applied to ensure that all of the different components were the same colour for the application of the base coat. The tank was based on a Marine 1st Tank Battalion Sherman as used in the Ryukyu Islands in mid-1945. The tank was painted in olive drab as outlined in Chapter 4. Stowage was added and the tank weathered. Crew figures from Milicast were added and the final touch was a bundle of logs that came from small twigs found in the garden that had been dried out. On the real tank these logs were used by the marines to fill holes, craters or anti-tank ditches, echoing the fascines used by tanks in World War I.

The Heller 1/72 scale M4A2, with OKB Grigorov tracks used to replace the soft plastic ones that came with the kit and added to the hull and turret sides.

The olive drab base coat was applied to the tank and then the tracks. Both those around the suspension and those welded to the hull and turret were painted in a suitable dull silver-grey.

Some twigs from the garden were dried and then made into a bundle with some brown cotton thread. The real tank had the bundle secured with rope, which had explosive cord attached so that the logs could be released by the crew without exposing themselves to enemy fire.

BUILDING THE M4A3 MEDIUM TANK

M4 A3 (75) in 1/48 scale

Bandai 1/48 M4A3 75mm Sherman Kit 8265

Hobby Boss 1/48 US M4A3 Medium tank 84803

RB M4 Sherman 75mm M3 gun barrel 48B05

RB 7.62mm Browning M1919 48B34

Black Dog 1/48 Sherman Deep Water Wading Trunks T48008

OKB Grigorov 1/48 tracks for M4 family T54E1

ABER etched parts for M4 Sherman (Early Production) 48003

Warlord US Marines Set WGB-A1-06

The Bandai kit is increasingly difficult to find these days and those that are available often command high prices. I was fortunate to pick up a number from a good friend at a very reasonable price. The hull, chassis and turret were built straight out of the box. The suspension units in the kit lack detail, so I replaced them with units from the Hobby Boss kit but kept the wheels from the Bandai kit. Tracks from OKB Grigorov were used and as with other kits the sprockets had to be widened by around 1mm, so the teeth lined up with the slots in the track. The tracks I used did not have grousers fitted, so I glued some in place from a different set of tracks. Plastic strip was cemented to the tank sides to provide support for the wooden veneer strips, which had been cut into planks to represent the spaced armour. It was at this point that I read that the US Marine Corps M4A3 (75) mostly had cupolas and so the split hatches of the Bandai kit were retrospectively replaced with a single hatch and cupola from the Hobby Boss kit in the commander's position.

With the build complete the model was given a coat of black primer and painted as set

The Bandai M4A3 kit provided the basis for the model with suspension units from the Hobby Boss kit. Although an old kit, the Bandai model needed only a small amount of filler.

The US Marine Corps M4A3 turrets had the later cupola with vision slots as opposed to the two hatches for the commander's position. Wooden laminate was added to replicate the wooden armour of the real tank.

The US Marine Corps camouflage schemes were more colourful than the olive drab seen on US Army tanks in Europe. Extra detailing included brush guards around the headlamps and a new bow machine gun.

out in Chapter 4. Whilst some US Army and Marine Corps tanks in the Pacific were finished in olive drab, some sported some more colourful schemes, which makes them interesting to model. This particular tank was based on a photograph of a 5th Tank Battalion tank landing on Iwo Jima in February 1945. Colours were based on Tamiya colours that were mixed to produce sand, earth red and olive green. Figures were added from the Warlord Wargames range and a simple base of grit resembling a sandy beach completed the diorama.

M4A3 (75) in 1/48 scale

Hobby Boss 1/48 US M4A3 Medium tank 84803

RB M4 Sherman 75mm M3 gun barrel 48B05

RB 7.62mm Browning M1919 48B34

OKB Grigorov 1/48 tracks for M4 family T54E1

Hauler Sherman M4 For Tamiya Set HLX48001

Tamiya US Army Infantry GI Set Item 32513

Warlord US Marines Set WGB-A1-06

The wading gear from Black Dog and the grousers on the tracks are seen to good effect here.

The next M4A3 to tackle was another US Marine Corps tank used in the Pacific. This was another 5th Marine Tank Battalion tank used at Iwo Jima but in a different scheme with different improvised armour. The Hobby Boss kit was the basis for this model. This kit is one of the more accurate Hobby Boss kits, but there are some errors. The engine deck is too wide, which throws out the fuel filler caps, but the model has a metal grille over the engine and sandbags around most of the upper hull and so these mistakes are hidden. The hinge detail on the front hatches is messy and so I removed this and replaced it with some plastic strip and the hatches with some from a Bandai kit that were a better fit. With the basic build complete, it was time to add the improvised armour. Like the other Marine Corps M4A3, this tank has

wooden planking on the sides but corrugated iron sheets gave extra protection and this was replicated using corrugated plastic card of a suitable pitch. Eduard fine mesh was used to provide the mesh covers that were fitted over the engine decking and hatches. Extra track links were cemented to the turret sides and etched-brass brush guards and periscope covers were added. The deep wading trunking was attached to the rear of the hull and the tank was painted as set out in Chapter 4. The scheme shown in Raymond Giuliani's *The Sherman in the Pacific War 1943–45* was followed, using Tamiya acrylics mixed to appropriate shades. The tank was placed on a base alongside a Japanese Tankette, which was 3D printed by Shapeways, and some figures that combined figures from the Tamiya set with some Warlord figures' heads and limbs.

The Hobby Boss M4A3 kit rear deck is not very accurate. However, this model was built as set out in the instructions, as the rear deck would disappear under some wire meshing and sandbags.

The hatches and transmission cover came from a Bandai kit. Filler was used quite extensively on this model. The corrugated iron side armour was added from embossed plastic card and glued onto some wooden laminate.

Sandbags from Miliput were added to the upper hull. The US Marines fitted their tanks with extra protection to deter infantry attacks by suicidal Japanese soldiers. The Japanese Tankette is a 3D-printed model from Shapeways. The photograph shows how tiny the Japanese Tankette was compared to the M4A3.

The USMC M4A3 next to the Japanese Tankette on a beach '...somewhere in the Pacific'. The background picture is from an old calendar.

M4A3 (105) in 1/48 scale

Bandai 1/48 US M4A3 105 mm Sherman. Kit 8288

Hobby Boss 1/48 US M4A3 Medium tank 84803

RB 7.62mm Browning M1919 48B34

OKB Grigorov 1/48 Tracks for M4 family T54E1

Hauler Sherman M4 For Tamiya Set HLX48001

Part M4 Sherman Fenders P48-002

The 105mm-armed Sherman looks quite different to the other M4A3, as apart from the obvious shorter and thicker main armament, the turret is quite different. I looked to add the Bandai turret to the Hobby Boss chassis, but having read that the rear deck of the Hobby Boss kit is not very accurate, decided to combine the rear of the Bandai hull with the front of the Hobby Boss kit. The fit

needed some filler to conceal the join, but the result was literally seamless. The suspension was from the Hobby Boss kit and the tracks from OKB Grigorov added. The gun mounting has a distinctive canvas cover over the rear of the mantlet and the turret front and this was made out of filler suitably shaped with a scalpel blade. Photo-etched details were added, as were the full-length track guards.

The tank was going to be finished in a winter scheme and I used the hairspray technique to achieve this. The M4A3 was sprayed in a grey primer coat and then given a base coat of olive drab from Tamiya. Once this was dry the decals were applied and then the entire model sprayed with hairspray to give the model an even coat. This was given a few minutes to dry and then sprayed with acrylic white to represent a thin coat of whitewash paint. An old stiff paint brush was dipped in water and then rubbed along the areas of wear around the turret edges and all of the hatches. Brown wash was then applied to the

The M4A3 used the Hobby Boss hull as the basis for the front part with a more accurate hull rear grafted on from a Bandai kit. Filler and the etched-brass side skirts helped to disguise the join between the two kits.

The 105mm Howitzer was mounted in a special mantlet that was fabricated using rolls of Miliput. The suspension units came from the Hobby Boss kit with tracks from OKB Grigorov.

whole model to tone down the remaining white wash. The steaking technique outlined in Chapter 4 was then applied, with the brush dragged down the hull and turret sides. Compacted snow was added to the suspension and sprinkled on the turret to represent fresh snow. The snow was from a Dio Dump kit and is a fine powder that was held in place with some diluted PVA glue. A tank commander from Dartmoor Models completed the model.

The tank was given a primer coat followed by a base coat of olive drab. Decals were applied and then the model was given a coat of hairspray. This coat is water soluble and coats of acrylic paint on top of this layer are easily rubbed off. The soluble hairspray layer gives a glossy sheen but this disappears under the acrylic 'whitewash'.

A thin layer of Tamiya white was sprayed over the model and then a stiff brush was dipped in water and rubbed vigorously in areas where the greatest wear would occur.

The Tamiya 1/48 kits are all superbly engineered, well detailed and easy to assemble. This kit of the M4A3 (76) W HVSS has a very modest part count and can be put together in a few hours to produce a modelling delight. I built this kit straight out of the box with only a few additions. The kit represents a very late version of the Sherman and this version of the tank has shot to fame because of

The crew climbing into the tank through the hatches would rub away the thin white wash revealing the olive drab base colour. Fresh snow was depicted as gathering in the folds of the mantlet cover and on top of the turret.

The finished model depicting a whitewashed M4 A3 105mm. Compacted snow was depicted around the wheels and suspension units.

M4A3 (76) W HVSS in 1/48 scale

Tamiya 1/48 M4A3E8 Sherman 'Easy Eight' Item 32595

RB 7.62mm Browning M1919 48B34

Hauler Sherman M4 for Tamiya HLX 48001 (including machine gun detailing)

Tamiya US Army Infantry GI Set Item 32513 (crew stowage)

Dartmoor Models US Army Crew

---

the film *Fury*. One minor gripe (and it is nothing more than that) is that instead of a metal chassis, as Tamiya produces on almost all other 1/48 tank kits, here they provide a plastic chassis with four short metal rods to add weight. The only changes I made were to enhance the turret casting surface by painting with Mr Surfacer 1200. I also added periscope covers from the Hauler detailing kit and some hatch handles from thin brass wire. The only other changes to the kit were to enhance the 0.5in calibre heavy machine gun with the Hauler detailing set and add a suitably long antenna from thin wire. Painting and weathering were completed as set out in Chapter 4 and the tank commander figure from Dartmoor Models replaced the Tamiya figure.

With the model painted, the final stage was to add stowage. The main load on the rear deck was made by wrapping some scrap plastic blocks in paper used to represent tarpaulins. These were made by taking a small section of some 80g white

The Tamiya M4A3 E8 model is unlike other 1/48 scale models from Tamiya, as it has a plastic rather than metal chassis. Metal rods are provided to add extra weight to the model.

The M4A3 E8 from the Bovington Tank Museum was used in the Brad Pitt movie Fury.

The kit was built straight out of the box. Mr Surfacer was used to depict the rough surface of the cast turret and small details were added from etched brass.

An atmospheric shot of the completed model. Allied tank crews realized that the white stars provided aiming points for German gunners and quickly painted over them as shown here on the turret.

paper and screwing it up into a tight ball. This was then smoothed out and painted in a suitable shade of olive drab. This was glued in place and some crates and jerry cans placed on top. The US Army used coloured panels in a variety of bright colours to provide an air recognition flag and one of these was made from some creased white paper and painted in acrylic orange. A thin masking-tape border finished off the panel. Bags and packs from a Hobby Boss kit were added, as was a hawser cable made from thin wire and terminated in the eyes from the kit's towing cable.

The final stowage was added to the front glacis plate. This consisted of a wooden plank made from balsa wood fixed between the front fenders with stowage piled behind it. The model was then fixed to a base made from a picture frame with some scenic grass given a light covering of artificial snow from the Citadel range.

The Friendship Models 'Jumbo Sherman' hull and turret kit is cast in resin and needs a suitable donor chassis to complete. I used the Hobby Boss M4A1 (76) W lower hull and suspension but discarded the 'rubber band' tracks and replaced

Stowage on the rear of the hull was tied down with ropes and a coloured canvas pane used for air recognition was added.

Etched-brass parts were used for the machine gun and the commander figure is from Dartmoor Models. The later versions of the Sherman were bigger than the original marks, but internal space was always at a premium, leading to crews stowing bulky items on the rear hull.

The base was made from a photograph frame. The completed model was positioned on a snowy base, depicting a vehicle in use during the winter of 1944–1945.

The M4A3 (76) W HVSS Sherman served at the end of World War II and later in Korea. It remained an important asset in many post-war armouries.

M4A3E2 in 1/48 scale

Friendship Models M4A3E2 Upper Hull and Turret

Hobby Boss M4A1 (76) W Kit 84081

RB 7.62mm Browning M1919 48B34

OKB Grigorov 1/48 Tracks for M4 family T54E1

Hauler Sherman M4 For Tamiya Set HLX48001

Tamiya US Army Infantry GI Set Item 32513

Warlord US Infantry Set WGB

them with an OKB Grigorov set that included grouser extenders. (The extra weight of the additional armour meant that all M4A3E2s were fitted with grousers to compensate.) I did briefly wrestle with the idea of squashing down the suspension units, as the extra weight did extend the springs of the Jumbo, but decided against it as in the smaller scales this is not particularly noticeable. The only surgery I completed was to replace the resin front mudguards with etched brass parts from the Hauler set. The model was painted and weathered

as outlined in Chapter 4 and then attention was focused on the infantry 'tank riders'. These combined the figures from the Tamiya US Infantry set with figures from the Warlord set.

The Hobby Boss Sherman chassis was used with the Friendship Models resin parts. The fit of parts is good, with just a little filler used to mate the photo-etched front mudguards with the hull.

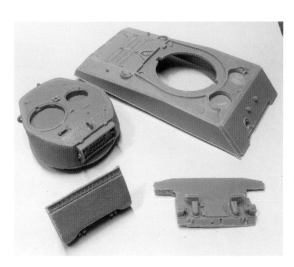

The Friendship Models 1/48 scale 'Jumbo' M4A3E2 consists of four resin parts that need to be mated to an injection-moulded kit chassis.

The infantry 'tank riders' were a combination of the Tamiya Infantry set and some figures from Warlord. The tank commander is from the excellent Dartmoor Models range.

The Warlord figures are designed for wargaming and are referred to as '28 mm' (1/56 scale) but are slightly oversized, so ideal to use with 1/48 scale armour.

US Marine M4A3 in 1/72 scale

Hull and hatches: Dragon M4A3(76) W VVSS
    Sherman, Armor Pro Kit 7567

Turret: Italeri Sherman

RB 75mm M3 gun

OKB Grigorov 1/72 tracks for M4 family

Part M4 Sherman Detailing set P72–121

Dragon is well known for their injection-moulded kits and have a vast number of kits in 1/35 and a smaller range in 1/72 scale. They tend to be at the expensive end of the spectrum but are normally high-quality kits. The 'Armor Pro' series of kits are cheaper than most Dragon kits, but the detailing is not as good as the more expensive kits. The chassis and suspension from the Dragon kit was used but the T23 Turret in the kit was replaced with a turret mounting a 75mm gun from Italeri. The Dragon tracks were disappointing. Dragon tracks are the traditional 'rubber band' style, but Dragon has patented a special plastic 'DS' for their tracks. These are very detailed and can be made to look as good as 'link and length' tracks, but the tracks in this kit are very thick and so I replaced them with tracks from OKB Grigorov. As we have already seen, the US Marine Corps painted some of their armour in unusual camouflage schemes and so, basing the scheme on information from *The Sherman in the Pacific War 1943–45*, I painted this model in a yellow and red scheme used by the 5th Marine Tank Battalion on Iwo Jima in 1945. The final additions to the tank were sandbags made from Milliput and nails from stretched sprue on the hatches.

The side wooden armour is real wood. Thin strips of wood used for veneering are available from good art shops.

Mig colours were used to represent the scheme used by the US Marine Corps tanks.

The ochre and red scheme of the US MC Sherman makes a change from the usual olive drab that the US Army tended to favour.

Chapter 8

Heavy Tanks

The US Ordnance Department finalized plans in October 1940 for a 50-ton tank with 75mm thick armour and coaxially mounted 3in and 37mm guns plus a top speed of 40km/h (25mph). Originally termed the Heavy Tank T1, this would develop into the M6A1. Problems with trials coupled with a shift from tank production to aircraft manufacture led to the planned production falling from 5,000 to 115 and ultimately only eight M6, twelve M6A1 and twenty M6A2s were built. None would see service, but they would be used for trials and evaluation of electric transmission systems and new guns.

The cancellation of the M6 programme was partially due to problems with shipping the tanks overseas. It made sense to transport two M4s rather than one M6 to the European and the Pacific theatres. US armoured doctrine often followed the German example, and in the early years of World War II German success was attributed to mass formations of medium tanks, so it was only logical that the USA concentrated on the M4 Medium Tank rather than the M6 Heavy Tank. However, the appearance of the German Tiger and, to an extent, the Panther, showed this logic to be flawed. Plans to replace the Sherman with a new tank had been in place as the first M4 Mediums rolled off the production line. The T20 series of tanks was plagued with difficulties but would culminate with the Medium Tank T26E1, which following trials in June 1944 became reclassified as the Heavy Tank T26E1.

The M26 Pershing was the forerunner of the US Army M48 and M60 Main Battle Tanks that served for many years as the mainstays of US Armored Forces. In the post-war world the M26 served in many NATO Armies. This example is in the Military Museum in Brussels.

In August 1944 the Ordnance Board recommended the T26E1 Heavy Tank should go into immediate production, but the Army Ground Forces insisted on more trials, leading to delays. All this would change when the inadequacies of the Sherman were demonstrated in the Ardennes when the German counter-offensive ripped through American armoured forces. Twenty T26E3s were rushed to Europe in January 1945 where it proved the equal of the German Tiger but far more reliable and manoeuvrable than the German heavy tank. The tank became standardized as the Heavy Tank M26 in March 1945 and served with distinction in Europe in the closing months of World War II.

BUILDING THE T26E3

T26E3 in 1/48 scale

Tamiya 1/48 M26 US Medium Tank Pershing
   Item 32537

RB 90mm Gun Barrel

RB 7.62mm Browning M1919 48B34

Hauler etched parts for M26 Pershing (Tamiya)
   HLX48176

The Tamiya T26E3 Heavy Tank is up to Tamiya's normal high standards. The only change I made was to the turret sides that had a coat of Mr Surfacer applied to emphasize the cast texture of the real thing. The other addition was to use most of the Hauler detailing set, which can be quite a challenge with the two part latches on the lockers a particular trial. Headlamp brush covers and periscope protectors are similar to those fitted on the Sherman as is the sighting frame. The turret-mounted storage rack looks much better than the kit part and is easy to form and fit. Once completed the model was sprayed with a primer coat of AK Ultra Black primer followed by a base coat of MIG 925 Olive Drab Dark Base. Highlights were picked out using MIG 927 Olive Drab Light Base before painting the tracks in my own mix of silver and dark grey track colour. Matt varnish and decals were applied and the model weathered as shown in Chapter 4.

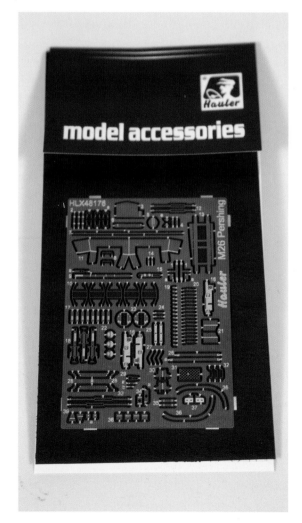

The Hauler M26 Pershing etched-brass detailing set contains a large number of parts to add detail to the Tamiya kit.

Elements of the Hauler detailing set added to the Tamiya M26. The turret-mounted stowage rack is much thinner than the plastic part supplied in the kit.

An overview of the finished M26 showing the cast effect enhanced using Mr Surfacer and the new turned-metal barrel and muzzle break.

The completed 1/48-scale Pershing from Tamiya. The tanks arrived on the front line still carrying the shipping stencils and this is faithfully reproduced on the Tamiya decal sheet.

Close up of the M26 turret showing the extra detailing that has been applied to the 0.50cal HMG. The figure is from Tamiya.

T26 in 1/72 scale

Pegasus 1/72 M-26 (T26E3) Pershing Heavy
  Tank No 7505

RB 90mm gun barrel

OKB Grigorov details for T26/M26 P72022

The Pegasus Pershing was originally marketed by Trumpeter and first released onto the market in 2010. The kit is in the middle price range and the detailing is crisp. Assembly is straightforward and I decided to use the tracks that came with the kit rather than the OKB Grigorov replacement tracks, as the kit tracks are nicely detailed and easy to

A Pegasus 1/72 scale Pershing showing some of the extra parts from the detailing set and the new 90mm gun.

A kit with the hull test fitted to the chassis. The hull, chassis, turret and tracks will all be painted separately and then assembled.

join together as they can be held together with normal plastic cement. The detailing kit has many small parts and I must confess that the tiny latch detailing on the lockers (a challenge in 1/48 scale as above) remained on the fret. The number of etched-brass kits available in the smaller scales of 1/72 and 1/76 is small compared to the larger scales and whilst some of the replacement parts are worth fitting, some of the smaller parts are difficult to fit and on the finished model are often invisible. As with all aspects of modelmaking, the level of detailing is up to the individual model-maker. Painting and weathering was completed as set out in Chapter 4.

The completed 1/72 Pershing from Pegasus. The etched-brass detailing set adds some small parts that enhance the completed model.

Chapter 9

Tank Destroyers

INTRODUCTION

As outlined earlier, the doctrine in the US Army shortly before the US entry into World War II was that armoured warfare would follow the Blitzkreig pattern, as practised to great effect by the Germans in 1939 in Poland and 1940 in France and the Low Countries. The concept of mass tank breakthroughs held sway, as did the plan to stop these massed ranks by the deployment of fast, lightly armoured but heavily armed tank destroyers. It was accepted that speed and high mobility were achieved at the expense of armour. Open-topped turrets and thin armour were essential to reduce weight, thereby ensuring this high mobility. A high-velocity weapon would ensure that the tank destroyer could dispatch the most heavily armoured enemy vehicle and, adopting 'shoot and scoot' tactics, the highly mobile tank destroyer would be out of harm's reach before the enemy realized where it had been.

Based on the knowledge at the time, the concept of the tank destroyer was sound. However, the Blitzkreig tactics of the early years of World War II gave way to slow slogging matches on the Eastern Front and more importantly for the Western Allies in Italy and initially northwest Europe after D-Day. The Germans tended to attack with all arms teams and the days of deploying armour en masse were over as the Germans ran out of men and machines to mount these massed tank attacks.

M6 37mm Gun Motor Carriage

The first US tank destroyer was the M6 37mm Gun Motor Carriage (GMC), which mounted a 37mm anti-tank gun in a Dodge ¾-ton truck. Although cheap to produce, this was a desperate and generally unsuccessful measure.

M3 75mm Gun Motor Carriage

The arrival of the M3 75mm GMC which mated a M1897A (the American version of the French '75' of World War I vintage) was much more successful than the M6 GMC and versions of this tank destroyer saw widespread service with US forces.

M10 Gun Motor Carriage

The most common US tank destroyers used the M4 Medium Tank chassis with a redesigned hull with thin armour and an open-topped turret, again with thinner armour than was found on the medium tanks in service. First of these was the M10 GMC that mounted the 3in gun that would have been fitted to the T1 Heavy Tank mounted on a M4A2 chassis. To increase production the M4A3 chassis was used to produce the M10A1. Numerically the most important tank destroyer used by US forces, its 3in gun would prove to be no match for the German Panther and Tiger tanks when they appeared. Despite this the M10 GMC stayed in front line service to the end of World War II.

A renovated tank destroyer being used by re-enactors.

© JOHN WOOLFORD

M36 Gun Motor Carriage

As early as October 1942 it was realized that the 3in gun fitted to the M10 would not be able to defeat the armour of the next generation of German tanks and so plans were started to fit an adapted 90mm anti-aircraft gun in an M10 GMC. Testing in March 1943 of an M10 fitted with a new turret mounting the 90mm gun were successful and the M36 GMC – sometimes referred to as the General Jackson – entered service in north-west Europe in October 1944. Its heavy hitting power made it very popular with tank destroyer crews, and the M36 GMC replaced the M10 GMC as more became available. To increase production the turret was mounted directly on an M4A3

Medium Tank hull to become the M36B1 and the M10A1 hull was also used with the 90mm turret to produce the M36B2.

M18 Gun Motor Carriage

The most successful US tank destroyer was an AFV designed specifically as a tank destroyer. This was the M18 GMC – known sometimes as the Hellcat, although this was never accepted as an authorized designation. The M18 had torsion-bar suspension and a Wright Continental R-975 engine that developed 400bhp. Given that the M18 weighed less than 20 tons, this powerful engine gave the M18 a maximum road speed of 89km/hh (55mph) making it the fastest tracked AFV in use by the

Name	Total built	Remarks
M6 37mm GMC	5,380	Initial attempt to produce a tank destroyer based on a soft-skin vehicle with 37mm gun
M3 75mm GMC	2,202	French 75mm gun
M10 3in GMC	4,993	3in gun mounted on M4 chassis
M10A1 3in GMC	1,413	As above mounted on M4A3 chassis
M36 90mm GMC	1,413	90mm gun. Most potent tank destroyer
M36B1 90mm GMC	187	As above on M4A3 chassis
M36B2 90mm GMC	724	As per M36 with turret mounted on an M10A1 chassis
M18 76mm GMC	2,507	Fast and effective tank destroyer

Allies. The main armament was the same 76mm gun used by the later versions of the M4 Medium Tank. The small size, low silhouette, high reliability and fast speed made the M18 popular with crews. Total losses in all theatres were 216 for 526 enemy AFVs destroyed – an impressive kill-to-loss ratio.

BUILDING US TANK DESTROYERS

An Italeri M3 75mm GMC painted in Pacific theatre colours. This is a simplified Wargames kit made up of only a few parts.

> **M3 75mm Gun Motor Carriage in 1/72 scale**
>
> Italeri M3 75mm Gun Motor Carriage –
>   Kit 7510

The M3 75mm GMC kit from Italeri is one of their simplified wargames kits that has two models in the box. The detailing is quite thick rather than crisp and there are numerous sink holes that need to be filled, but generally this is a good model that is ideal for wargaming and needs only a small amount of detailing to make a reasonable collector's display model. The 'On The Way!' website (www.onthewaymodels.com) has information on how to add more details to this kit. I added suitably modified figures from the Fujimi M3A1 kit and Milicast and painted the model in camouflage colours as seen in the Pacific theatre of operations.

> **M10 Gun Motor Carriage in 1/56 scale**
>
> Italeri M10 Tank Destroyer No 15758

Aimed squarely at the wargames market, the kit has sixty-three parts, which is an unusually high number for a wargaming model. However, the suspension and tracks come in seven parts each side, which makes assembly easy for the inexperienced or junior modelmaker. Unusually for a wargames model, the kit comes with crew figures, hatches that can set open or closed and a comprehensive decal set. Assembly is straightforward and the assembled model was given a primer coat of coat Vallejo Surface Primer USA Olive Drab 70.608. The model was completed in olive drab with figures placed inside the open turret ready for the wargames table.

An Italeri 1/56-scale (28mm) M10 was given a primer coat of Vallejo Surface Primer.

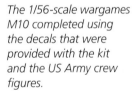

The 1/56-scale wargames M10 completed using the decals that were provided with the kit and the US Army crew figures.

M36 Gun Motor Carriage in 1/72 scale

Armourfast M36 Jackson No 99025

Friendship Models (Wee Friends) M10 Detailing and interior set WVC 72113

Black Dog 1/72 M-10 Accessories Set No T72079

RB 90mm gun

The Armourfast kit comes as two quick-assembly models. Built straight out of the box the M36s look reasonable and certainly acceptable for the wargames table. However, only a small amount of work is needed to upgrade the model to make it look more realistic. The Friendship Models set provides a turret basket with ammunition stowage, gun breech and a new turret front. I fitted the RB turned-metal gun to the kit mantlet. The side stowage racks were also from the spares box and these were fitted alongside a set of scratch-built track holders. Simplified headlamp protectors and lifting brackets were added from brass rod. The process of painting this M36 is comprehensively covered in Chapter 4. Once painted, some elements of the Black Dog stowage set were added, as were two figures.

The Armourfast M36 with turret interior details from Friendship Models. Stowage racks are from an old Nitto kit and the gun barrel is a metal one from RB.

The appearance of the Armourfast M36 is improved by the addition of stowage racks. The stowage on the rear is from Black Dog.

A complete M36 put on a base and ready for the wargames table.

M18 Gun Motor Carriage in 1/72 scale

Armourfast M18 Hellcat No 99034

Friendship Models (Wee Vehicle Resin
    Conversions) M18 Hellcat Conversion WVC
    72118

The Armourfast M18 in 1/72 scale and the
Milicast M18 in 1/76 scale are the only small-scale
kits of this important allied tank destroyer available.

The Armourfast kit is a quick-assembly wargames
model with limited details. The Friendship Models
set provides a turret basket and a hull interior,
both in resin. The basket needs some surgery so that
it fits inside the turret, but this is straightforward
and worth the effort. The only other change was
to add headlamp and siren protectors and two
small brackets to the hull front from plastic scrap.
Finished in olive drab, two crew figures were
added, as was additional stowage to disguise the
baskets on the turret sides.

The Armourfast M18 fitted with the turret interior from Friendship Models and brush protectors from brass rod.

The modified M18 on a suitable base and ready for the wargames table. The 1/72 scale M18 Hellcat from Armourfast has extra detailing, interior details and crew figures added.

Chapter 10

Howitzer and Gun Motor Carriages

INTRODUCTION

As outlined in Chapter 2, with the success of the German Blitzkrieg in Europe the US Department of Field Artillery realized that traditional horse-drawn artillery was desperately in need of replacement by either motor tractor or self-propelled mounts. We will briefly examine armoured artillery tractors in the final chapter, but will concentrate here on the main Howitzer and Gun Motor Carriages that saw service with US forces during World War II.

Howitzer Motor Carriage T30

The M3 Half-track was used to carry a variety of weapons and the success of the M3 75mm Tank Destroyer persuaded the US Ordnance Department to fit a 75mm Howitzer M1A1 in an M3. Regarded as a stop-gap measure, a total of 500 were ordered, with 312 being delivered and the remaining 188 converted back to M3 Half-tracks. The T30 was used in North Africa, Sicily and Italy in HQ Companies of Armored Divisions until replaced by the fully-tracked M8.

Howitzer Motor Carriage T19

The heaviest weapon mounted in the M3 Half-track was the 105mm Howitzer M2, to produce the Howitzer Motor Carriage T19. The layout was similar to the T30 and 324 were built, which were mainly used in Tunisia. A few T19s were used in

Sicily and Italy and as part of the US invasion of southern France. Declared obsolete in July 1945, most had been replaced by the M7 Howitzer Motor Carriage long before then.

Howitzer Motor Carriage M8

Work on a fully-tracked self-propelled gun had begun in early 1941 and after a number of false starts combining the M1A1 Howitzer in a new open turret with an M5 Light Tank resulted in the T17E1. The design was changed little to produce the first M8 Howitzer Motor Carriage, which would appear in September 1942. This vehicle was sometimes known as the 'General Scott'. A total of 1,778 M8s were built before production was phased out in January 1944, with the 105mm-armed M4A3 Medium Tank replacing the M8 HMC in Medium Tank Battalion HQs. They were used in Italy and the early phases of the campaign in north-west Europe as well as in the Pacific theatre.

Howitzer Motor Carriage M7

The T19 HMC had demonstrated that combining an existing AFV with an in-service field artillery piece enabled the artillery to keep up with the advancing armour. However, the need for an AFV that was better protected and more mobile than an overladen half-track led to fitting in the chassis of a medium tank (in this case the M3 Medium) the standard 105mm calibre howitzer, resulting in the Howitzer Motor Carriage M7 in February

1942. Full-scale production began in April 1942 and would continue until July 1945. The change of standard Medium Tank from M3 to M4 resulted in the M7 changing to reflect this with the M7B1 based solely on the M4A3 Medium Tank chassis. Total production reached 3,489 M7 HMC and 826 M7B1s. This AFV served in the artillery battalions of all American Armored Divisions throughout World War II and some were employed in the Korean War. Examples remained in front-line service with the Israeli and West German armies until the 1960s.

Gun Motor Carriage M12

The US Ordnance Department had considered plans to fit the French-designed World War I 155mm M1918 guns in a tracked chassis as early as June 1941. But the US Army considered that they would have little use for such a large-cali-bre weapon in a self-propelled mount. However, undaunted, the Ordnance Department pushed on with development and by fitting the 155mm gun on a modified M3 chassis produced the M12 Gun Motor Carriage in August 1942, with 100 produced by March 1943. The US Army remained unconvinced of the value of the M12 GMC and they were initially used only for training in the USA. However, in another twist of fate, by December 1943 with invasion of Europe looming the army

relented and asked for seventy-four M12s to be overhauled and made ready for deployment. Used in Europe mainly for indirect firing missions, the M12 also acquitted itself well when used in direct-fire tasks against fortifications such as the Siegfried Line.

Motor Carriage M40

With the M12 being prepared for the invasion of Europe, the Army Ground Forces Board looked to fit a 155mm M1 gun or an 8in M1 Howitzer in a heavily modified M4A3 Medium Tank chassis. The resulting M40 Gun Motor Carriage was rushed into service, with a few examples featuring the 155mm gun and an 8in howitzer serving in the European theatre as World War II ended.

BUILDING US ARMY SELF-PROPELLED GUNS

T19 105mm Howitzer Motor Carriage in 1/76 scale

Fujimi M3A1 Halftrack Kit 38042
Revell M7 Priest Kit 03216 – 105mm Howitzer
Revell M16 Halftrack Kit 03228 – mudguards

A T19 based on the Fujimi half-track with the 105mm gun from the Revell M7 kit.

The Fujimi kit with front mudguards from the Revell kit formed the basis of the model. The drawing from George Bradford's *Allied Armored Fighting Vehicles: 1:72 Scale* was used as the guide for adding the 105mm Howitzer from the Revell M7 kit. The figures are from a variety of sources, including the Fujimi (formerly Nitto) M4 Sherman kit, which includes a figure that looks remarkably like a figure from the old Airfix Paratroopers and a second who resembles an Airfix US Marine bazooka loader. Both figures are in hard plastic and so were easy to alter to make the T19 crew figures.

Glasgow-based Milicast produces an enormous range of World War II vehicles in resin. Built to a constant 1/76 scale, the majority of models come either ready built or with a minimum number of parts. Designed with both wargamers and collectors in mind, the breadth of models available is unparalleled in small scale. In the Milicast Premier Range there are 106 American models, the Battlefield Range has fifty American vehicles and there are twenty different American figure

sets available. The M8 HMC is not untypical of the Milicast range. Separate front hatches, gun breech and mantlet, as well as a two-part turret and single-part hull make up the model. The hull interior is nicely detailed.

The Revell kit is the old Matchbox kit re-boxed. First released in 1979, the kit is a simplified version of the M7 HMC; however, with a little work it builds into a neat replica that will please both the wargamer and serious collector. I drilled out the barrel and added a new HMG as well as headlamp brush guards and some stowage front and rear. Despite being of the 'rubber band' type, the tracks are nicely detailed and fit well. Matchbox devised a means of joining the tracks by slotting them together that does not need glue, staples or cotton thread. The figures that come with the kit are neatly posed and I used two of the three. The kit includes some shells to fit in the rack, but they do not look right – and from the photos that I have seen most of the rounds were kept in fibre-board tubes until used. The Nitto kit is now available as a Fujimi kit

---

M8 Howitzer Motor Carriage in 1/76 scale

Milicast Battlefield Series M8 Howitzer Motor Carriage BA 054

M7 105mm Howitzer Motor Carriage in 1/76 scale

Revell M7 HMC 'Priest' Kit 03216
Nitto M7B1 105mm Gun Kit 454

The Milicast M8 HMC in 1/76 scale is a resin model that needs little assembly.

The Nitto (nearest camera) and Revell M7 HMC. The Nitto kit is the later version (M7B1) with the M4 suspension, as opposed to the earlier M7 with M3 suspension.

M12 Gun Motor Carriage in 1/48 scale

Gaso.line Canon automoteur GMC US M12 155mm Ref GAS48063

Tamiya 1/48 M4 Sherman Item 32505

ABER etched parts for M4 Sherman (early production) 48003

Tamiya WWII US Willy's jeep with set of nine figures Kit 32552

Warlord US Infantry (WW II American GIs) No 402013012

(kit 72218) and builds into an accurate version of the later type of M7 HMC with the M4 chassis. The suspension is the weakest part of the kit, with the wheels undersized. I replaced the tracks with some from the spares box as the kit ones are very soft, vinyl-type plastic that look awful.

The Gaso.line kit contains the upper hull and 155mm gun in resin and needs a suitable chassis and suspension with the recommendation in the instructions that a Tamiya M4 is used as the donor. The Tamiya kit was built as set out in the instructions and the resin upper hull was a good fit on the Tamiya chassis. The only additions were some brass rod bent to make loop handles and a strut on the deployed spade. The kit includes a box on the left-side superstructure – I believe used to hold spare track links – that was very delicate in thin resin, so I replaced it with a box made from plastic card. Headlamps came from the Tamiya kit and etched brass brush protectors from the ABER set. The model was to be displayed in the firing position and so the recoil spade was cemented in the down position. The completed model was painted in olive drab and suitably weathered to depict an M12 in a deployed position with the spade suitably muddy.

The Gaso.line M12 in 1/48 scale fits well on the Tamiya Sherman kit. The resin kit has well-detailed parts which are to the same standard as some injection-moulded kits.

A rear view of the completed model showing the recoil spade that is well reproduced on the Gaso.line model.

A close-up view of the crew figures that are a combination of figures from Tamiya and Warlord.

The gun-crew figures were built in suitable poses by combining the Tamiya figures with some heads and limbs from the Warlord set. The Gaso.line kit comes with some 155mm shells and the two figures at the front of the diorama are seen setting the fuses on these shells. Once set the prepared shells are laid down on a canvas cover ready to be loaded. The spade on the M12 was lowered into position with a winch and some cotton thread was used to represent the hawser and was strung through the pulleys on the model. One figure was depicted adjusting one of these pulleys. The model was set on a base made from a picture frame with the two small chocks from the kit fitted underneath the tracks at the front. A small collection of items was added to finish off the diorama.

> **M12 Gun Motor Carriage in 1/72 scale**
>
> Italeri M12 Gun Motor Carriage Kit 7076

The Italeri M12 kit can trace its roots back to 1975, as that is when Esci first released the original kit. It has been re-boxed and re-released by numerous manufacturers since – including Revell, Polistil, Humbrol, ERTL and Gunze Sangyo – and has never been out of production. This latest version from Italeri was released in 2019, which is a great testimony to the quality of this kit. Once completed you can see why, as despite being fifty

The deployed M12 with figures from Tamiya, Dartmoor Models and Warlord.

The ramps are nicely portrayed in the kit and were used on the real M12 as part of the recoil system, to reduce the effects of firing the enormous gun.

The figures in the foreground are priming the 155mm shells and prepared shells are laid down on a tarpaulin.

years old, the kit detail is crisp and flash free which suggests the moulds have been refurbished probably many times.

I built this kit very much straight out of the box. The tracks are link and length and the fit of parts is generally very good. I did struggle with the rear spade, as the instructions do not look much like the parts. However, this quibble aside, it does produce a neat replica and the choice of decals means you can build four different vehicles. The only additions I made were to depict the breech open by adding some detailed parts from scrap plastic and adding a single marker pole to the kit part from a long, suitably painted metal pin.

The Italeri 1/72 scale M12 builds into an accurate and well-detailed kit with decals for four different vehicles.

The completed Italeri M12 using the decals provided in the kit to depict an AFV from B Battery, 557th Armoured Field Artillery Battalion, in Germany in 1945.

M40 Gun Motor Carriage in 1/76 scale

Revell M40 GMC Kit 03280

First released in 1978 by Matchbox, the M40 kit was re-boxed and re-released by Revell in 2019. I built the kit out of the box and added some stowage and a hawser to the front of the AFV that is depicted in travelling mode.

The Revell M40 GMC is a re-boxed Matchbox kit. The model is very simplified and therefore suitable for Wargamers.

Chapter 11

Half-Tracks and Multi-Gun Motor Carriages

The M3 Half-track armoured personnel carrier was widely used by the US Army and Marine Corps in every theatre throughout World War II. The half-track concept sought to combine the cross-country agility of a tracked vehicle with the road mobility of a wheeled vehicle. Initially the vehicle was unpopular due to being open topped, but found favour as World War II progressed. However, after World War II most countries rejected the half-track concept in favour of fully-tracked infantry carriers.

Developed in the 1930s, the T14 became standardized as the half-track M2. This was the artillery tractor, and by lengthening the vehicle hull and other modifications it became the M3 Personnel Carrier. The M3 had a pedestal mount for the 0.50in-calibre HMG. This was replaced in 1943

© JOHN WOOLFORD

Renovated US Army half-tracks are a popular subject for armour enthusiasts. This one was seen at a Military Vehicle Rally at IWM Duxford.

Type	Manufacturer	1941	1942	1943	1944	Total
M3	White, Autocar, Diamond T	1,859	4,959	5,681		12,499
M3A1				2,037	825	2,862

with a ring-mounted 'pulpit' to accommodate the armament to produce the M3A1. As well as a successful artillery tractor and personnel carrier, the half-track was a stable platform for a variety of weapons.

The T54 Gun Motor Carriage was an attempt to mount a 40mm Bofors anti-aircraft gun onto an M3 half-track. Two pilot models, the T54 and T54E1, were built but trials showed that the platform was not stable. A revised version, the T59, was produced with outriggers fitted, but this was superseded by the more successful M19, featuring mounted twin Bofors guns on the M24 Light Tank chassis. Only one version of a 40mm Bofors mounted on an M3 half-track saw service and this was termed the M15 'Special'. A number of these were built by the US 99th Ordnance Depot in Australia and deployed to Luzon before seeing service in Korea.

The most successful anti-aircraft version of the half-track was the series known as the Multiple Gun Mount Carriage (MGMC). The M13 MGMC mounted twin 0.50cal machine guns in a Maxson turret on the M3 and this was up-gunned by the addition of a 37mm Gun Carriage M3E1 with repositioned 0.50cal guns in a turret to produce the M15 and M15A1 MGMC. A new Maxson turret that mounted four 0.50cal HMGs was fitted to the M3 to produce the M16 MGMC.

The half-track was adapted to carry the 81mm mortar with the converted M2 and M2A1 known as the M4 and M4A1 respectively. The M3 had more room internally, so was used to produce the 81mm Mortar Carrier M21. The major change compared to earlier versions was that the mortar could be fired forward from the vehicle.

As well as the need for artillery, the US Army recognized the need for a tank destroyer. An expedient design was to mount the M1897A 75mm gun on a forward-firing pedestal in the M3 Half-track. Designated the 75mm Gun Motor Carriage M3 (T12), despite the hurried design and development of the weapon it proved successful in trials and examples were rushed to the Pacific and North Africa. When replaced in the US Army these vehicles were passed to the British, who used them in Italy though to the end of World War II.

BUILDING THE HALF-TRACK IN US SERVICE

M3A1 in 1/76 scale

Airfix Vintage Classic M3 Half Track – Kit A02318V

Revell M16 Halftrack – Kit 03228

M3A1 in 1/72 scale

Forces of Valor 1/72 US M3A1 Halftrack #873007A

The Airfix M3 half-track first appeared in 1966 and is still available. The kit is based on the M14 and so has a few inaccuracies, but these can be easily addressed. The interior is sparse and, after putting most of the kit together, I used plastic card to add seats and internal detail based on some photographs in Steven Zaloga's *US Half-tracks of World War II*, published by Osprey. The main difference between the M3 and M3A1 was the mounting for the 0.5in cal HMG. In the latter version this was in a pulpit to the right of the driver's position, whereas in the former the HMG was fitted on a pedestal mount. The other change was to replace the straight front mudguards with the more curved ones of the Revell (formerly Matchbox) kit. The pulpit was modified with a brass rod added as a support and the internal edge of the pulpit adapted to better resemble the real thing. The Forces of Valor kit is one of a small range of plastic kits from a Chinese company that is probably better known for its die-cast models. The model looks quite accurate – although the detail is quite heavy – but it makes a neat model that can be used by wargamers or serious collectors alike.

The Academy kit contains an M3A1 half-track, an amphibious Jeep and a Harley-Davidson motorbike. For this conversion the kit was put

An Airfix M3A1 half-track. Most of the work involves the internal seating and the kit mud guards are replaced with ones from the Revell M16 kit.

The completed Forces of Valor half-track is a good budget-end model. The M3A1 is shown here with infantry figures that came from various sources.

40mm Bofors mounted on an M3 half-track

T54 40mm Gun Motor Carriage in 1/72 scale

Academy M3 half-track and [¼] ton Amphibian kit 13408

Zvezda British Bofors 40mm MkI/II AAG Kit 6170

Dan Taylor Modelworks Bofors gun barrel

T54 40mm Gun Motor Carriage in 1/76 scale

Revell M16 half-track – Kit 03228

Airfix Bofors 40mm Gun & Tractor Kit A02314V

M15 'Special'

Revell M16 half-track – Kit 03228

Airfix Bofors 40mm Gun & Tractor Kit A02314V

Dan Taylor Modelworks Bofors gun barrel

together as per the instructions up to the end of Stage 4. A new cab rear and rear frame were

added from layers of plastic card. The Airfix Bofors kit donated the base of the Bofors gun, which was shaped to accept the Zvezda gun and fitted onto the rear chassis. The Bofors gun was put together with the only change being to replace the barrel with a turned-brass barrel from Dan Taylor Modelworks. With the assembly complete the model was painted with primer followed by olive drab with the seats, footrests, handles and rounds picked out in appropriate colours. A single white star was applied to the bonnet before the vehicle was weathered as set out in Chapter 4. I built a simpler version some years ago from a Revell M16 (although it was probably a Matchbox kit), coupled with an Airfix Bofors gun. The M15 'Special' was built combining the Revell M16 and the Airfix Bofors gun, with a Dan Taylor metal gun barrel, all fitted inside a scratch-built turret. Completed in olive drab, the model was weathered and then two crew figures were added in the cab.

The Revell M16 was first released in 1974 under the Matchbox label and was re-boxed under the Revell brand in 1996. The model is about 2mm

The Academy half-track is modified to take the Zvezda 40mm Bofors gun. The rear is mainly scratch-built with the supporting ring from the Revell M16 kit suitably modified.

Although part of a wargames 'Art of Tactic' series, the Zvezda Bofors is an accurate kit. A 40mm gun barrel from Dan Taylor Modelworks has been added.

A front view of the T54, showing the extra detailing added from plastic rod with headlamps from the spares box.

A completed T54 on a small base with a crew figure from the Revell (formerly Matchbox) US Infantry set.

Another T54 built in 1/76 scale from the Revell M16 and Airfix Bofors set.

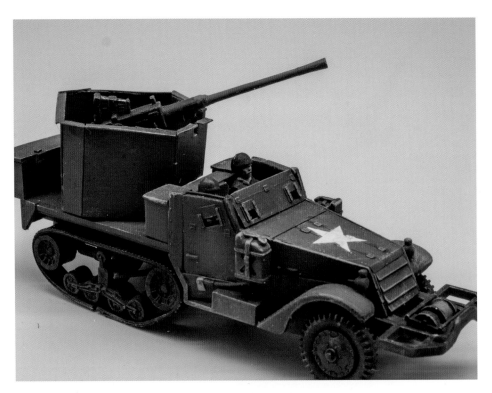

The M15 'Special' used the Revell M16 with the Airfix Bofors gun in a scratch-built turret.

Multiple Gun Carriage M14 in 1/76 scale

Revell M16 half-track – Kit 03228

Fujimi M3A1 half-track – Kit 38042 – turret and guns only

M21 81mm Mortar Carrier in 1/76 scale

Fujimi M3A1 half-track – Kit 38042

Revelll M16 half-track – Kit 03228 – mudguards

---

too narrow, but overall it captures the look of the original and I built one straight out of the box with the only changes being to add extra details to the Maxson turret rear. The M14 was a simple conversion that used the twin HMG Maxson turret, which comes with the Fujimi kit. All of the multiple gun carriages had partial fold-down sides and rear to enable the guns to depress. I added strips of plastic card to the M14 to enhance the detail on the kit. The only other change was to hinge the front armoured plate in the raised position with a thin strip of plastic card and support struts added. The M14 was painted in olive drab and weathered with two figures added.

The Fujimi M3A1 kit is very similar to the Airfix M3 kit and repeats some of its mistakes. The most obvious error is the mudguards, so the only major change is to replace the Fujimi mudguards with those from the Revell kit. For the M21 Mortar Carrier, the internal layout was rebuilt from plastic card based on some articles on the 'Warlord Games' website (store.warlordgames.com). Photographs of the real vehicle show a ladder-like storage rack on the sides of the M21, and these were added. An 81mm mortar was put together from a number of sources and three crew figures were added. The model was painted in olive drab as outlined in Chapter 4.

A Revell (formerly Matchbox) M16 built virtually out of the box. Extra detailing has been added to the Maxson turret rear.

The M14 is a simple conversion that uses the twin HMG Maxson turret with the Revell M16.

The completed M14 with the Revell US infantry figure that has appeared elsewhere.

An M21 mortar carrier in 1/76 scale. The main changes are to the internal layout of the model.

The completed mortar carrier with a crew from a variety of sources and an 81mm mortar from a US infantry set.

Chapter 12

Other Armoured Fighting Vehicles of the USA

INTRODUCTION

As well as fully-tracked tanks, half-tracks, tank destroyers and various gun and howitzer platforms (both single and multiple), the US Army and Marine Corps used a variety of other armoured vehicles during World War II. In this chapter we will briefly examine some of the armoured cars, artillery tractors, armoured Jeeps and Landing Vehicles Tracked as used by the US forces. The chapter ends with a look at some of the US vehicles that went no further than a prototype.

© JOHN WOOLFORD

A restored M8 Armored Car manned by re-enactors at a recent War and Peace Show.

ARMOURED CARS

The M8 Light Armored Car was originally planned to be used as a tank destroyer, but experience with the Dodge truck and 37mm as the M6 GMC persuaded the US Army to use the vehicle in a scout and reconnaissance role. With a good road speed and fitted with reliable long-range radio, the M8 was employed by cavalry units and excelled in this role. The M20 was a turretless version of the M8 that was primarily used as a Command Vehicle. The M8 saw action with the US Army in Sicily in 1943 and was subsequently used in Italy, northwest Europe and the Pacific theatre of operations.

ARTILLERY TRACTORS

As we saw earlier in the chapters about Howitzer and Gun Motor Carriages and in the section about the 105mm-armed Sherman, the US Army in World War II had a number of half-track and fully-tracked self-propelled artillery guns. However, in addition towed artillery, field guns, heavy guns and howitzers, anti-tank guns and anti-aircraft artillery were all a major part of US Army and Marines armouries. Most artillery tractors were un-armoured but some were used in service tank chassis to provide a means of towing the guns or keeping the guns supplied with ammunition.

M30 Cargo Carrier

The M12 served as the basis of the M30. The major difference was the removal of the gun and recoil spade. The M30 Cargo Carrier carried 155mm ammunition, stores and gun crew. There was one M30 for each M12 in the field and the M30 Cargo Carriers were an essential part of each M12 Battery.

M34 Prime Mover

The M34 Prime Movers were the M32B1 Recovery Vehicle (*see* below) without the towing cable and were used for pulling heavy artillery, such as the 240mm Howitzer, into position.

M35 Full-Track Prime Mover

Removing the turret and machine guns from a standard M10A1 and fitting a compressor unit, pintle assemblies, front and rear and four additional seats resulted in the M35 Prime Mover. Used mainly to tow the 8in M1 gun and the 240mm Howitzer M1, the M35 saw service in northwest Europe from late 1944.

M39 Armored Utility Vehicle

A modified M18 GMC Hellcat chassis became the T41 Armored Utility Vehicle. Standardized in early 1945 as the M39, a total of 650 were built and the type was used as the prime mover for the 3in Gun M5. The M39 saw service in the last few months of World War II in Europe.

M32 Tank Recovery Vehicle

There were numerous specialist vehicles based on the Sherman chassis and one of the most successful was the M32 Armored Recovery Vehicle. Fitted with a 5.5-metre A-frame jib and a 30 (short) ton winch, the M32 entered service with the US Army in July 1943 and served throughout World War II and beyond. Different versions of the M32 appeared based on different versions of the M4 Medium Tank, as shown below.

M32 – Based on the M4 Sherman. 163 were produced by Pressed Steel Car in 1944.

The M32 Armored Recovery Vehicle was used by the US Army in the second half of World War II. Model in 1/35 scale by Simon Ward.

M32B1 – Based on the M4A1. 1,085 were produced by Federal Machine, Baldwin Locomotive, and Pressed Steel Car.

M32B2 – Based on the M4A2. 26 were produced by Lima Locomotive.

M32B3 – Based on the M4A3. 344 were produced by Lima Locomotive and Pressed Steel Car.

M32B4 – Based on the M4A4 but never entered production.

M32A1 – An M32 but with HVSS suspension.

M32A1B1 – As M32B1 above but with HVSS suspension. 175 were converted by Baldwin Locomotive.

M32A1B2 – As M32B2 but with HVSS suspension.

M32A1B3 – As M32B3 but with HVSS suspension.

ARMOURED JEEPS

The US Army Truck, ¼-ton, 4×4, Command Reconnaissance, better known as the Jeep, was the most widely used vehicle of World War II. Whilst there were never any armoured Jeeps manufactured on the production line, a few were adapted to carry additional weapons behind an armoured shield. Perhaps the most extraordinary was the rocket jeep, which carried two banks of six 4.5-inch rocket tubes. An armoured roof and windscreen provided some protection for the crew. Only used in very small numbers, the impact on the enemy was perhaps more psychological than destructive.

Attempts to rationalize field modifications led to a kit of plates of thin armour being sent out to some units so that a three-sided armoured box could be added to the Jeep to provide some protection against small arms fire. But the extra weight had a significant impact on mobility and the modification was never that popular. However, some units added extra protection to their Jeeps and their use during the Ardennes Offensive was noteworthy.

LANDING VEHICLES TRACKED (ARMORED)

Before the outbreak of war the US Marine Corps had been looking to develop a vehicle suitable for amphibious operations. The Alligator was a civilian tracked vehicle developed for use in the swamps of the Florida Everglades. Working with the designer of the Alligator, the Marine Corps developed the Landing Vehicle, Tracked LVT 1 as an unarmoured cargo carrier. A larger version – the LVT 2 – was in use when the USA entered World War II.

US LVTs

US Army experience in the Pacific theatre led to a whole series of armoured troop carriers and amphibious tanks based on the original LVT-2. These are listed below.

LVT-1

The first military model capable of carrying up to twenty-four fully-equipped assault troops to the beach, this vehicle was armed with initially two 0.30cal machine guns and later two 0.50cal Browning machine guns in the front and two 0.30cal guns aft. The LVT-1 was not armoured and proved to be very vulnerable; 1,225 were produced.

LVT-2 (British designation Buffalo II)

This model was very similar to the LVT-1, with a new power plant taken from the M3A1 Light Tank and 'torsilastic suspension' – suspension arms consisting of several concentric tubes with a rubber-based filler between the tubes; 2,962 were produced.

LVT(A)-1

Based on the LVT-2, this fire-support version had an armoured (6–12mm) hull. It was fitted with a turret nearly identical to that of the M5 Light tank with a 37mm gun and two rear-mounted machine guns. 510 were produced.

LVT(A)-2 (Water Buffalo)

Armoured version of the LVT-2 with a capacity to carry eighteen troops; 450 were produced.

LVT(A)-3

Armoured version of the LVT-4, never approved for production.

LVT-3 Bushmaster

Developed by the Borg Warner Corporation, this vehicle had engines moved to sponsons and a ramp installed in the rear similar to the LVT-4. Some were armoured. First used in Okinawa in April 1945; 2,964 were produced.

LVT-4 (Water Buffalo British designation Buffalo IV)

The engine was moved forward and a large ramp door was added to the rear, allowing troops to exit down the ramp rather than having to clamber over the sides of the LVT. This innovation also greatly facilitated the loading and unloading of cargo. Some vehicles were armoured. It was by far the most numerous version of the LVT, with 8,351 units delivered.

LVT-4(F) Sea Serpent

British version armed with flamethrowers.

LVT(A)-4

Similar to the LVT(A)-1, this heavy-support version was armed with a 75mm howitzer in an M8 turret. A single 0.50cal machine gun was installed on the ring mount above the turret rear. In the late-production vehicles the heavy machine gun was replaced with two M1919A4 0.30 MGs on pintle mounts and one more in the bow mount. Some versions had a Ronson flamethrower fitted instead of the howitzer; 1,890 were produced.

US ARMY EXPERIMENTS

One genre of military modelmaking that has recently blossomed, as reflected by the number of kits available, is the 'Paper Panzers' set of models, depicting AFVs that would go no further than a single prototype or perhaps even only ever existed as a drawing in the design office of a German tank manufacturer in the final stages of World War II. Some are pure fantasy and the fascination with such designs is understandable.

Other nations flirted with designs that would never progress into production, with the USA having one of the most prolific outputs. Even as the Sherman medium tank was entering production, the Americans realized that a well-armed and heavily-armoured heavy tank would be needed to take on German heavy tanks that were rumoured to be in production. In line with Europe (albeit a little behind), the Americans considered multi-turreted behemoths. Such a design was the T1 Heavy Tank that would eventually become the M6, M6A1 and M6A2. Tipping the scales at around 56 tons (coincidentally the same weight as the German Tiger), none of these giant vehicles ever actually saw action. This was because US armoured doctrine at the time focused on fast medium tanks and so, although a total of forty M6 models were built, none was deployed. Their contribution to the story is that the M6 was used as a base for experiments that would eventually result in the M26 Pershing (see Chapter 8).

Alongside the development of a heavy tank, the M4 Sherman was also coming to fruition, as we saw in Chapter 7. However, even before the first Sherman had been delivered off the production line, the US Office of the Chief of Ordnance proposed that an improved M4 should be considered. The result was a layout drawing that came from the Aberdeen Proving Ground, demonstrating a Sherman-like medium tank that had sloping armour front and sides, tracks much wider that the M4 and a powerful Wright G200 air-cooled radial engine that developed 640bhp. This superseded the power of the Sherman M4 Continental R975, which only developed up to 400bhp. This new design was in many ways superior to that of the production M4 Sherman and to some extent resembled the Russian T34 – perhaps the best tank deployed in World War II. The armour of the new design was thicker than that carried by the Sherman and, as it sloped, would have offered a significant improvement in protection over the M4. The wider tracks reduced the ground pressure to below that of the Sherman and the new suspension would eventually evolve into the HVSS suspension of the late-war M4s. One weakness in the design was the turret, which it was proposed should carry the standard 75mm M3 medium-velocity gun. Another more serious design flaw was the re-location of the fuel tanks to under the turret ring. This combined with carrying the main armament rounds in the sponsons (as in the Sherman), meant that the mooted new, improved Sherman would be just as vulnerable to catching fire as the M4 Sherman. Ultimately the design went no further than an artist's impression – but it makes for an interesting modelling project.

The M4 also proved to be an ideal platform for experiments with a vast number of other designs to carry a variety of weapons and perform numerous roles. The 'Funnies' built for the British 79th Armoured Division are well known, but the US Armored Forces also developed special-purpose vehicles to tackle obstacles such as minefields, anti-tank obstacles and enemy bunkers. Many were based on the M4 chassis and, whilst some were delivered in significant numbers – such as the M32 Recovery Vehicle and M34 Prime Mover – others like the T1E1 Mine Exploder (known as 'Earthworm') and T1E3 Aunt Jemima would be

The 'Aunt Jemima' T1E3 Mine Exploder. Based on the UM kit, new suspension units from an Italeri kit were used and a scratch-built structure added to the rear.

produced as only 'limited procurements'. The vast majority of these experiments would end up as single examples that would – often for good reason – go no further than one or two prototypes. Typical of these is the T31 Demolition Tank, which carried two 7.2in rocket projectors on each side of a dummy 105mm howitzer in a heavily armoured turret.

T23 MEDIUM TANK

On 25 May 1942, five months before the Sherman made its combat debut at El Alamein, the US Ordnance Department began to look for a new medium tank to replace the M4. Given the provisional designation M4X, a series of pilot models were built that would become the T20 series of tanks. Various pilot models were built in parallel, but only the T23 pilot built by the Detroit Arsenal in January 1943 would go into production. A 'limited procurement' of 250 tanks was built between November 1943 and December 1944, but none would see combat. In many ways the T23 was superior to the M4 that it was designed to replace. Featuring a lower silhouette than the Sherman, a roomy turret mounting a high-velocity 76mm gun, a new HVSS suspension and a clean 47-degree front glacis plate, these were just a few of the

advantages that the T23 had over the Sherman. However, poor weight distribution and concerns over the revolutionary electric transmission would seal the fate of this tank.

Nevertheless, the T23 was a test bed for many of the features that would be used to improve the Sherman tank. The T23 turret had the same size turret ring as the M4 and so was easily fitted to a variety of Sherman models, including the M4A1, M4A2 and MM4A3. These Shermans also adopted the 47-degree glacis and some had the HVSS suspension fitted. Further developments of the T23 would lead to the T26, which would enter service in the closing stages of World War II as the Pershing. This model would further go on to become the M26, which was used to equip US Armored Forces after World War II (see page 159).

THE T31 DEMOLITION TANK

It often seems that unusual and experimental tanks were the domain of German armour – particularly in the final stages of World War II. As mentioned previously, 'Paper Panzers' are a popular subject for modelmakers, with more fantasy variants of the 'Maus' available than genuine Allied armour such as the Cromwell. The Americans did experiment with mine clearers and flame tanks and, whilst most got no further than prototypes, there are examples that went into limited production and made a contribution to the war effort.

The T31 Demolition Tank fits firmly in the prototype category and is a most unusual-looking AFV. In November 1944 the Joint Army–Navy Experimental and Testing Board (JANET) met to consider an armoured vehicle that would be used by engineers to demolish structures. The resulting design was named the T31 Demolition Tank and three pilot models were requested. Design layouts were produced in January 1945 and the first pilot was completed just as World War II ended in August 1945.

Based on an M4A3 hull with HVSS, the all-new turret had two T94 7.2in rocket launchers with a revolver-type loader that held five rockets. Two 0.30-calibre machine guns were mounted in the turret front below a dummy 105mm howitzer barrel. Whether the dummy gun was a mock-up with the intention of a working 105mm ultimately being fitted is unknown, but the prototype was fitted with attachments for an M1A1 bulldozer blade as well as a 50-gallon flamethrower unit in the right sponson. Trials at the Aberdeen Proving Ground did not go well, and with the end of hostilities funding for the T31 dried up and the project was cancelled with no further prototypes being built (see page 163).

SHERMAN 'E' SEARCHLIGHT TANK

When it comes to unusual specialist armour, the British led the way in World War II. For the invasion of Europe the 79th Armoured Division used specialist armour – known as 'The Funnies' – to great effect both on D-Day and in the subsequent push across Europe. One of the most secret of these tanks was titled the Canal Defence Light (CDL) and consisted of a powerful carbon-arc light mounted in a turret that would illuminate enemy positions and could be made to flicker to disorientate the enemy. The CDL was demonstrated to US officials in 1942 and initial enthusiasm for the CDL

(code-named 'Leaflet' by the Americans) led to 497 tanks being produced by 1944. These were based on the M3 Medium and the US Army looked to fit a new searchlight turret with a 75mm gun alongside the light to the M4. Design work started in May 1944 and a single prototype based on a large hatch M4A1 was completed in January 1945. But with the war in Europe drawing to a close, the project was abandoned. However, in 1950 the project was revived in response to a request from the US Eighth Army in Korea and plans were made to develop the T52 searchlight tank. Sadly these were ultimately shelved, due to the high cost of a new development in relation to simply fitting standard M4s with unprotected searchlights.

M35 in 1/72 scale

Armourfast 1/72 scale M36 Jackson No 99025

Friendship Models (Wee Vehicle Resin Conversions) M10 WVC 72

Hauler M1 8inch Gun Transp.wagon HLP72016

M39 in 1/72 scale

Armourfast 1/72 scale M18 Hellcat No 99025

Friendship Models (Wee Vehicle Resin Conversions) M39 Armoured Utility Vehicle WVC 72113

ACE 1/72 scale US 3 inch AT Gun M-5 on Carriage M-6 Cat #72531

The Armourfast kit is designed for wargaming, so there is no internal detail in the hull. The Friendship Models M10 set was used with the ammunition racks removed. The Armourfast wheels and tracks are cemented to the hull. Whilst the tracks are simplified, the one-piece suspension is ideal for fitting to the Wee Vehicle lower hull. The Armourfast hull was detailed with headlamp guards and storage racks from an old Nitto kit. A half-circle cover from embossed plastic card was added to the open compartment and stowage from a variety of sources was added to the hull rear and sides once the model had been

The Armourfast M36 formed the basis of the M10 Artillery Tractor. Used to tow the 8in and 240mm heavy artillery guns, the model takes up a lot of space, even in 1/72 scale.

painted. The Hauler M1 8inch Gun on transport carriage is a resin kit with photo-etched detailing. Even in 1/72 scale it is a monster and looks good towed behind the M35.

The Friendship Models M39 set consists of an internal detail part and an upper hull, both provided in resin. The Armourfast M18 chassis and suspension are cemented to the Friendship Models kit and hatch covers, with machine-gun

ring and spare tracks from the Armourfast kit added. Side stowage racks assembled from brass rod were added to the sides of the hull and simplified headlamp protectors were also made of brass rod. Figures from a variety of sources were added to make the crew. The towed 3-inch anti-tank gun was quite a challenge to build and I added an RB turned-brass gun barrel.

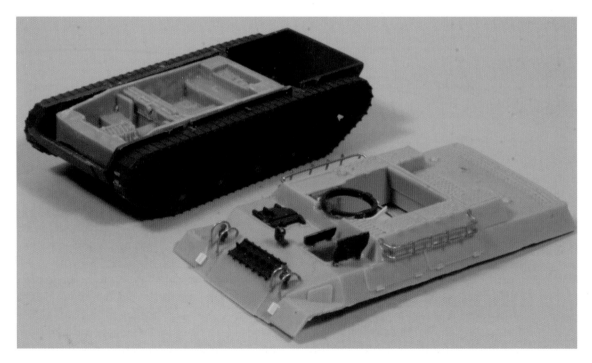

The M18 Hellcat chassis is the basis for the M39 Utility Vehicle that consists of an internal detail set for the lower hull and an upper hull, both from Friendship Models.

The completed M39 Utility Vehicle completed in olive drab with crew figures and stowage from a variety of sources. The M39 was used in the closing stages of World War II but was extensively employed post-war.

Rocket-Launching Jeep in 1/48 scale

Tamiya 1/48 scale WWII US 'Willy's' jeep with set of 9 figures Kit 32552

Black Dog 1/48 scale Jeep Rocket Launcher No T48027

Rocket-Launching Jeep in 1/72 scale

MisterCraft 1/72 scale ¼ Ton Truck 'Willy's' Kit D-299(042998)

Esci 1/72 scale US M4 A1 Sherman Calliope No 8059

Armoured Jeep in 1/48 scale

Tamiya 1/48 scale WWII US 'Willy's' jeep with set of nine figures Kit 32552

Hauler 1/48 scale Armored Jeep (82nd Airborne Division) No HLX48210

One of the frustrations of building kits in 1/48 scale is that even common vehicles are overlooked or expensive to buy. Such is the case with the most common 'soft skin' of World War II – the Jeep. Tamiya do produce a model of the ubiquitous ¼ Ton Light Truck, but it is part of a set that includes nine figures. Although some of these figures could be used with the Jeep, this is an expensive way to buy a reasonable Jeep in 1/48 scale. However, the kit goes together easily and the fit of the Black Dog rocket tubes is straightforward. The figures from the Tamiya set were suitably posed and the model was secured to a small wooden plinth on some brick paper from a model railway scenery supplier. The only addition I made was to add the catches and detail to the rear of the tubes.

The Rocket Jeep in 1/72 scale used the Jeep from MisterCraft. I believe this was the Heller kit originally, and this or the latest from Airfix in 1/72 scale would be suitable. The rocket tubes I used were from a very old Esci kit that is harder to source, as the Esci kit has not been available since the 1980s and the re-boxed version from Italeri went out of production in 2008. The rocket tubes in the Airfix Sherman Calliope kit could be

The Tamiya Jeep formed the basis of the Rocket Jeep in 1/48 scale. The Black Dog rocket tubes and frame fit easily to the kit.

A rear view of the Rocket Jeep, showing to good effect the Black Dog rocket tubes. Extra detail was added to the rear of the tubes.

used, but are nearer 1/76 than 1/72 scale. They are quite easy to produce from plastic tube, as outlined with the 1/48-scale Sherman Calliope in Chapter 7. The Jeep was built very much as set out in the instructions with the windscreen not fitted. A frame was cemented into the rear of the Jeep from brass rod and plastic card. The rocket tubes were assembled with a thin band of plastic card wrapped around them and glued to a plastic card base. The armoured cab was fabricated from plastic card with some brass rod bent to replicate the front shield mount. With the model completed, it was given a coat of primer and olive drab.

The Mistercraft limited-edition kit formed the basis of the 1/72 Rocket Jeep. Scratch-built frames to support the tubes were built using brass rod.

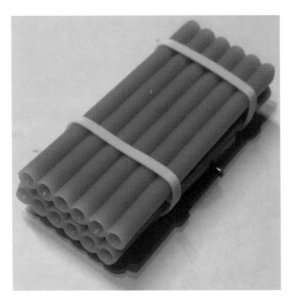

The rocket tubes were from an old Esci Sherman Calliope kit, but plastic tubes of the right dimensions could be used.

Kits for troops to build Armored Jeeps in the field were provided in real life and the 82nd Airborne Division used these to great effect during the German Ardennes Offensive in December 1944 to January 1945. For the scale model, the Tamiya 1/48-scale Jeep was used as the basis with the Hauler detailing set added. The etched brass armour plates are easy to fold and fitted well inside the Tamiya kit.

The converted Rocket Jeep in 1/72 scale, showing the scratch-built armoured cab.

The completed 1/72 Rocket Jeep. The armoured cab would provide some protection – but being inside that cab when the rockets were fired must have been quite exciting…!

The Tamiya 1/48 scale Jeep with the etched-brass set from Hauler to make an Armored Jeep.

The assembled Jeep with a 0.5cal Browning machine gun with the thin etched-brass armoured plate front and sides.

Snow chains were made from some scale chain that I had in the spares box.

The completed Armored Jeep of 82nd Airborne Division, as used in the Ardennes. A thin coat of whitewash has been applied, as seen on many US vehicles during the Battle of the Bulge.

LVT 4 in 1/72 scale

Dragon LVT – 4 Water Buffalo Kit 7389

Photographs of some Jeeps used during the fighting in the Battle of the Bulge show Jeeps fitted with snow chains, so I added these using some scale chain from Tank Workshop. I chose to produce the version armed with a 0.50cal HMG and added a figure from the Tamiya set to complete the model.

Die-cast models have come a long way since the days of Dinky and Matchbox. Nowadays, some injection-moulded kit manufacturers produce assembled models that are either a combination of plastic and metal or just die-cast metal. Hobby Master (also known as Altaya/IXO) produces a die-cast LVT-(A)1 that I believe was part of a magazine series of 1/72 scale models. Whilst the model has a toy-like sheen that can be easily disguised with an oil-paint wash, Dragon also produces a small range of die-cast models as well as their extensive range of kits in 1/72.

The Dragon LVT-4 is the very late-war version that was built straight out of the box. Dragon have a great reputation for kit making in all scales and many of their 1/72 kits are the finest on the market. However, one problem I did encounter with this particular kit was the tracks. Dragon launched a new material for tracks known as 'DS'. These tracks are made of a soft plastic but are highly detailed and can be made to realistically follow the contours of the drive sprocket and idlers. (These are areas where many 'rubber band' tracks typically fall foul.) These DS tracks were packed in a sealed plastic bag, but taking them out of this packet they emerged covered in an oily liquid and were so brittle that they snapped into numerous pieces. I used the tracks from another Dragon LVT to complete this model. In an attempt to salvage the original tracks, I soaked them in warm soapy water. After drying them off I found that they were more flexible and will probably be all right to use with the other kit. A trawl of fellow modellers revealed that this was an isolated incident, but perhaps something to look out for if you regularly build Dragon kits. I painted the model in olive drab and heavily streaked the side sponsons to depict a vehicle that had been in and out of the Pacific on many occasions.

Hobby Master LVT-(A)1 is a die-cast model that looks toy-like until the application of a suitable wash and some streaking down the sides.

The Dragon LVT-4 built out of the box with the decals provided in the kit. Streaking along the side sponsons was heavily done to depict a well-used AFV.

The Dragon kit represents an AFV that was used in the final stages of the war in the Pacific.

The ramp-lowering hawser provided in the kit was brittle and snapped in several places whilst fitting and so was replaced with some stretched sprue.

MODELLING THE T23 MEDIUM TANK

Hobby Boss US M4A3 (76) Tank 84805
(turret, engine deck and suspension)

OKB Grigorov Tracks T48 with two extended
end connectors Type 1

Aber US 76mm M1A2 barrel 48L-26

RB 7.62mm Browning M1919 48B34

Hauler etched parts for M4 Sherman
HLX48001

Plastruct plastic sheeting 0.25mm, 0.5mm and
1.0mm thickness

Whilst the T23 would not see active service, this tank would make a significant contribution to the development of US armoured forces. Ironically the Sherman that the T20 series was designed to replace would be the greatest beneficiary of the development of the T23 and the lineage of the M26 is clear to see. Despite this pedigree there is no large-scale model manufacturer that makes a model T23 in any scale. To address this I decided to scratch-build my own version of the T23.

The model is based on the drawing on page 85 of R. P. Hunnicutt's *Sherman: A History of the American Medium Tank*. The drawings in this splendid book are all in 1/48 scale and generally very accurate. I started off by cutting the turret ring out of the Hobby Boss kit and cut a sheet of 1.0mm plastic card to form the front and sides of the chassis. I installed a strengthening rib to support the turret ring and rear engine deck. The next stage was to cut out the engine deck from the Hobby Boss kit and fit to the rear deck, which had been fabricated from plastic card. A fuelling cap was added from the kit in the centre of the engine deck and the top mudguards added to each side. The Hobby Boss turret was measured up against the drawings and found to be accurate with only a few minor tweaks required. I installed the Aber metal barrel through the kit mantlet in the turret and the escape hatch was replaced with a small oblong of plastic card. The turret construction was completed with some etched brass detailing, an antenna base and two small stubs in front of the

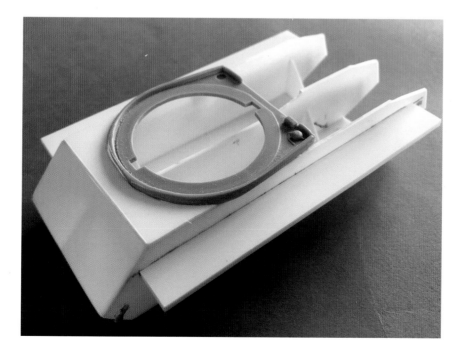

The T23 was built mainly from scratch using plastic card. Extensive use of internal ribs ensured the model was strong and not liable to warp.

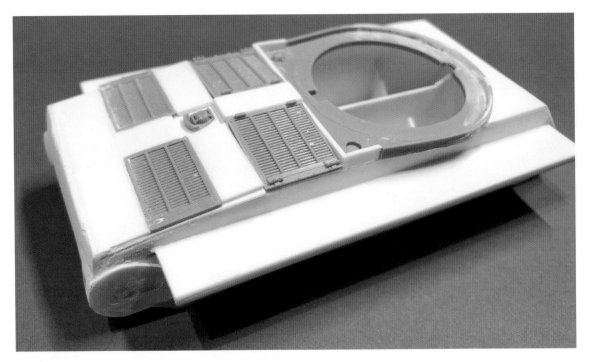

Parts from the Hobby Boss kit were used for the turret ring and the engine louvres.

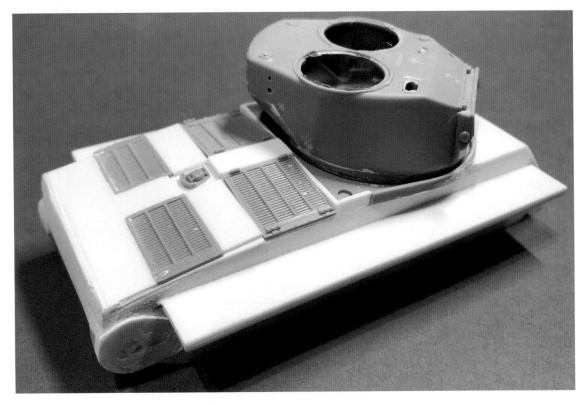

The turret from the Hobby Boss kit provided the basis for the T23 model.

The suspension units from the Hobby Boss kit provided the basis for the T23. These were carefully positioned following the drawings in the R. P. Hunnicutt book, Pershing: A History of the Medium Tank T20 Series. *The drive sprockets were enlarged to take the wide OKB Grigorov tracks. A turned-metal gun barrel was added to the mantlet.*

The rear of the hull is a distinct curve and was made using the aluminium from a takeaway container.

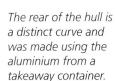

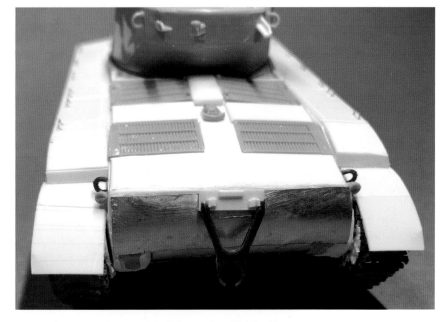

Parts from an etched-brass set provided the extra details, such as the handles on the side lockers and the headlamp guards.

The T23 model is a combination of parts from an injection-moulded Hobby Boss Sherman kit, some scratch-building using plastic card and details from an etched-brass set.

loader's hatch. Using the components from the Hobby Boss kit, I then fitted the VVSS suspension units. The drive sprocket and idlers were from a Bandai kit with the sprocket width increased to accommodate the OKB Grigorov tracks. The tracks were then added and the side lockers over the mudguards. The rear part of the chassis is a complex curve and I used some of the thin aluminium from a takeaway tray to form the curve. The fine detailed parts – including the locker handles, periscope cover and hull machine gun – were all added at this stage.

With the construction complete, the model was given a coat of AK Black Primer. The model was sprayed in MIG 925 Olive Drab Dark Base with highlights added using MIG 927 Olive Drab Light Base. The tracks were painted silver grey and the tyres on the wheels painted dark grey. Decals were added from the spares box before the model was given a coat of matt varnish. Weathering was kept

to a minimum as the real vehicle was only used for limited trials.

The Rubicon kit is designed primarily for wargaming and so is simplified in construction. Unusual for a wargames model there is a choice of turret (early or late production T23) and suspension (T48, T54E1 with Duckbill extenders or HVSS), so it is possible to make an M4A3 or M4A3E8. There are only sufficient parts for one tank, but the spare parts can be useful for converting other models. Another unusual feature is the inclusion of an additional M2 HMG, which is called 'modeller version' and has a slimmer barrel than the wargames version. The kit goes together easily as you would expect and the detail is better than on the average wargames AFV.

The turret was an experiment with 3D printing. I found the software program for the T31 turret as a free issue on the internet and sent the order to Shapeways to print off. I chose the best standard

The scratch-built T23 Medium Tank with a Dartmoor Models commander figure. The serial number represents one of the first early-production tanks.

Although never used in anger, the T23 made a significant contribution to US Armored Forces through the 76mm armed turret that was fitted to the Sherman and as a test bed for some of the components that would be used in the M26 Heavy Tank.

T31 Demolition Tank in 1/56 scale

Tank hull: Rubicon Models M4A3E8 Kit
   280042

Turret: Shapeways 3D-printed

The 3D-printed T31 turret. The ribs on the front are a result of the 3D printing process and were rubbed down on the finished model.

material, which pushed the price up considerably and the turret ended up costing around twice the price of the Rubicon kit. The turret measured out to around 1/59 scale, so a little undersized but acceptable for a wargames model. The rocket launchers and dummy 105mm were solid and too brittle to drill out, so I replaced them with brass tube and a suitable length of sprue. The commander's hatch and 0.5in cal HMG were from the kit and a circle cut from plastic card for the turret ring completed the model.

The real T31 never entered service so I decided to model the tank in a factory finish and to do this I followed a guide that Vallejo recommend on their 'AFV Painting System'.

PAINTING THE T31

To replicate a factory finish I followed a technique that is different to that shown in Chapter 4. It is equally applicable to any US Army and Marine AFV.

A new technique

All the paints you need – albeit in small 225ml (8oz) bottles – are in the US Olive Drab AFV Painting System from Vallejo Item 78406.

Primer

The primer coat is in olive drab using Vallejo #608. This coat is applied using an airbrush set to 20psi with the airbrush held 10cm from the model.

The T31 Demolition Tank was given a coat of Olive Drab Surface Primer from Vallejo.

Shadows

In Chapter 4 we looked at spraying a black primer and then spraying thin layers of base colour, with the aim of having the black primer just about visible in the recesses to replicate shadows in these areas. Using an olive drab primer means that you have to add the shadows and Vallejo #013 Yellow Olive is recommended by Vallejo.

Shadows on the T31 were emphasized by spraying the recessed areas with Vallejo #013 Yellow Olive.

Areas of the T31 that were more prominent were airbrushed with Vallejo #016 US Dark Green. Vallejo #043 Olive Drab was sprayed over the most prominent areas, following the guidance from the Vallejo AFV painting scheme.

Highlights

The Vallejo set includes two olive drab colours (#016 and # 043) that are applied in the more prominent areas of the tank to produce highlights. I used the airbrush set to 10psi around 5cm from the model.

Raised details

The next stage in the Vallejo System is to highlight raised details using Vallejo #044 Light Grey Green. I used a fine point brush (size OO) to pick out periscopes and other raised detail.

Varnish

The final stage is to coat the model with Vallejo #522 Satin Varnish.

Weathering, filters and washes

If you are aiming to replicate a vehicle that has just come off the production line or has been made ready for a parade, then you need go no further. However, the vast majority of vehicles do not have this 'showroom' finish and I felt that even though the T31 had not been used on active service I wanted to tone down the olive drab and applied a thin filter and light pin wash. I stopped at this point, but if you want to weather your vehicle further then details are to be found in Chapter 4.

A green filter was applied over the whole model to tie together the different shades and a light pin wash used to emphasize the panels and recessed areas.

> **T31 Demolition Tank in 1/72 scale**
>
> Tank hull: Hasegawa M4 A3 E8 Kit 31115
> Turret: UM T-31 Demolition Tank No 456

The 1/72 scale Hasegawa Sherman M4A3E8 is a strange kit, as the hull is around 3.5mm too long and 0.7mm too wide. Conversely, the UM kit is around 1.5mm too short and the suspension very complicated (twelve parts per bogie), so I decided

The Hasegawa M4A3 E8 upper hull is around 3mm too long and the area behind the turret ring is where the problem lies. The chassis at the bottom of the picture has been shortened compared to the untouched chassis above it.

The different-coloured plastics show the variety of kits used to produce an accurate version of the T31 in 1/72 scale.

to shorten the Hasegawa body and use the UM wheels with the simplified Hasegawa suspension. The Ukraine-based manufacturer UM covers a vast number of subjects in small scale; the assembly of the numerous parts (often without locating pins and holes) can be challenging. Consequently, the hull for this model was mainly from the Hasegawa modified with UM parts. This was completed by the addition of the UM link and length tracks rather than the 'rubber bands' in the Japanese kit.

The completed T31 Demolition Tank with a dozer blade from the UM M10 kit added. Although the real tank did not have a dozer blade fitted, it is likely that if the T31 had entered service as an engineer vehicle a dozer blade would have been added.

M4A1 Sherman Searchlight in 1/48 scale

Tank: Hobby Boss US M4A1 (76) W Medium Tank Kit 84801

Tracks: OKB Grigorov Tracks for M4 1/48 scale

Turret: K Scale Models M4A1 Sherman CDL type E

Although the T31 never saw active service, there is speculation that in the Engineer role the tank could have been fitted with a dozer blade and so I added one from another UM kit. The model was painted using the technique outlined above for the 1/56-scale model and then mounted on a small base.

The Hobby Boss kit was built very much out of the box with the only changes being to replace the tracks in the kit with some from OKB Grigorov. (*See* Chapter 7 for more details.) The turret is from K Scale Models, who offers a small range of military conversion kits and items for model railways. Although part of only a limited range, the searchlight turret is of an exceptional standard. These are early days for 3D printing, but I have little doubt that in the future 3D-printed models will replace resin for conversion kits and detailing sets for military models. This model has none of the 'ridging' that is often seen as part of the 3D printing process and the detailing is as good as you would find on an injection-moulded kit. Prices for 3D printed models are high, but doubtless this will change as source materials and the prices of high-quality printers reduce.

The Hobby Boss 1/48-scale M4A1 with the K Scale Models Type 'E' searchlight turret.

Close up of the 3D-printed turret. Parts produced this way are more expensive than the equivalent plastic or resin parts and so are not yet that popular.

A close-up of the armoured searchlight. Unlike the British army, the US Army did not use the armoured searchlights in action and plans post-war to re-activate the programme were shelved due to cost.

Selected Bibliography

There are many thousands of books on military history and military modelmaking and probably many hundreds feature the US Army and Marine Corps in World War II. Below are some of the books that I have used for reference and inspiration. (Arranged in alphabetical order by author's surname.)

Name	Author	ISBN	Remarks
Allied Armored Fighting Vehicles 1:72 Scale	George Bradford	9780811735704	Set of drawings of the most numerous allied AFVs. Other books in the series cover larger scales.
British and American Tanks of World War II	Peter Chamberlin and Chris Ellis	1845090098	Encyclopaedic guide to allied armour. First published in 1969 but still a generally accurate history of allied armour.
Small-Scale Armour Modelling	Alex Clark	9781849084147	The essential guide for the serious 1/72 scale modeller. No US Army AFVs featured, but the best book on the subject on the market by far.
US Marine Corps 1941–45	Mike Chappell and Gordon Rottman	1855324970	Osprey Elite Series 59.
Sherman Tank Volume 1	David Doyle	9780764355677	First volume in the series that looks in great depth at the Sherman. This volume looks at the M4A1.
Sherman Tank Volume 2	David Doyle	9780764358470	Second volume in the series. This book examines the M4 and M4(105) Medium Tanks.
M7 Priest	David Doyle	1526738856	Part of the *Images of War* series, with some rare photographs.
M12 Gun Motor Carriage	David Doyle	1526743523	Part of the *Images of War* series, with some archive photographs and a good set of a museum-based M12.

M36/M36B1 Tank Destroyer	David Doyle	1526748924	Part of the *Images of War* series, showing the US Army tank destroyer in archive photographs.
Sherman. The M4 Tank in World War II	Michel Esteve	9781612007397	A superb guide to some of the more obscure aspects of all M4 Medium Tank variants.
US Army Handbook	George Forty	0750932104	Good general guide from the well-regarded George Forty.
US Marine Corps Handbook 1941–1945	George Forty	0750941960	Good overview of the US Marine Corps in World War II.
Medium Tank M4 (76mm & 105mm) Sherman and Firefly	Terry J. Gander	0711029897	Part of the *Tanks in Detail* series, with numerous photographs.
Sherman in the Pacific War 1943–45	Raymond Giuliani	9782352502838	Comprehensive guide to the Sherman in the PTO. Hundreds of photographs and some excellent colour plates showing side views of the Sherman. Hard to find but worth the effort.
Modelling and Painting World War II US Figures and Vehicles	Ray Haskins	9781785007156	Comprehensive guide for wargamers.
Sherman: A History of the American Medium Tank	R. P. Hunnicutt	9781626548619	The definitive guide to the M4 Medium Tank. Authoritative history with numerous scale drawings in 1/48 scale.
Pershing: A History of the Medium Tank T20 Series	R. P. Hunnicutt	9781626541672	The definitive guide to the T20 Medium Tank and M26 Heavy Tank. Authoritative guide that includes many scale drawings in 1/48 scale showing the development of the T20 series.
M2/M3 American Half-tracks of the Second World War	Robert Jackson	1526746557	Part of the *Land Craft Series* from Pen and Sword. History of the real vehicle with some nicely finished models.
How to Paint 1:72 Military Vehicles	Mig Jimenez and various authors	8432074060192	Superb guide from a variety of modelmakers. No US Army vehicles of WWII are featured but the various techniques are applicable to US AFVs.
How to Paint WWII USA ETO Vehicles	Mig Jimenez	8432074065005	Solution Book 1 from master model maker Mig Jimenez. Features exclusively Mig Ammo products – inspirational.
Painting Wargaming Tanks	Mig Jimenez and Ruben Torregrosa	8432074060031	The recent revolution in painting military vehicles has been led by Mig Jimenez. Ideal guide for wargamers.

US Marine Corps – Uniforms and Equipment in World War II	Jim Moran	1526710412	Comprehensive guide to the US Marine Corps.
Sherman Tanks: US Army North-Western Europe, 1944–1945	Dennis Oliver	1526741865	Part of the *Tank Craft* series from Pen and Sword. Excellent history with colour illustrations and some well-made and painted models.
M4 Sherman	Pat Ware	1781590294	Good general guide to the iconic M4 Medium Tank.
US Infantryman v German Infantryman	Steven J. Zaloga	9781472801371	Steven Zaloga is a deservedly world-renowned master modelmaker and US Armour authority. Osprey *Combat* series with some excellent drawings of US infantry.
US Half-tracks of World War II	Steven J. Zaloga	0853686971	*Tanks Illustrated* 15. Full of excellent reference photographs.
US Half-tracks of World War II	Steven J. Zaloga	0850454816	Classic Osprey Vanguard 31.
The Sherman Tank in US and Allied Service	Steven J. Zaloga	0850454271	Osprey Vanguard 26. First published in 1982, but still relevant with some good colour plates.
Modelling US Armor of World War 2	Steven J. Zaloga	9781846033988	Definitive guide to building and painting US armour in 1/35 scale.
Modelling the US Army M4 (76mm) Sherman Medium Tank	Steven J. Zaloga	9781846031205	An excellent guide to building and painting the M4 (76mm), mainly in 1/35 scale with a 1/48-scale model included.
Modelling the US Army M4 (75mm) Sherman Medium Tank	Steven J. Zaloga	9781841769653	Volume 35 in *Osprey Modelling* series. Inspirational guide to building the M4 in 1/35 and 1/48 scales.

Index

Modelling British World War II Armoured Vehicles
Tom Cole
ISBN: 9781785005473

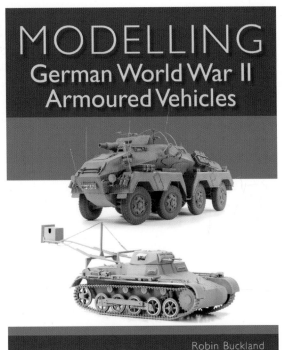

Modelling German World War II Armoured Vehicles
Robin Buckland
ISBN: 9781785005152

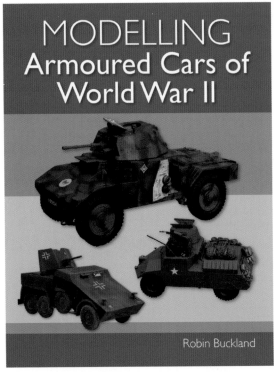

Modelling Amoured Cars of World War II
Robin Buckland
ISBN: 9781785009068

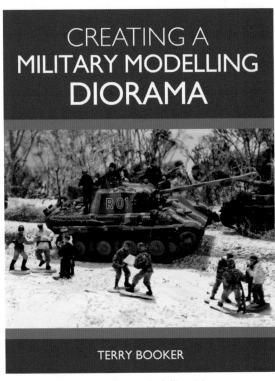

Creating a Military Modelling Diorama
Terry Booker
ISBN: 9781785009044